Children's World ATLAS

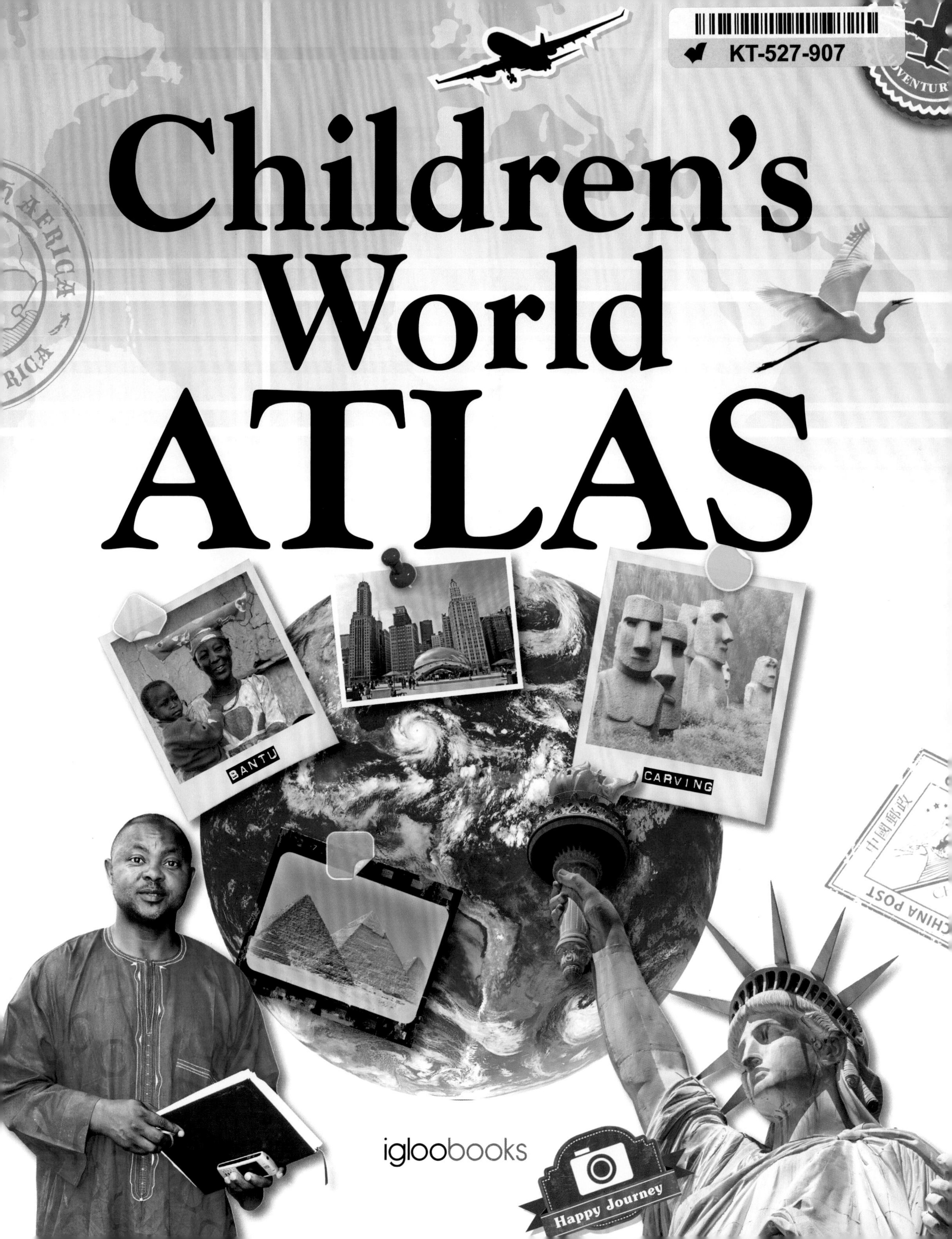

igloobooks

igloobooks

Published in 2013
by Igloo Books Ltd
Cottage Farm
Sywell
NN6 0BJ
www.igloobooks.com

SHE001 0713
2 4 6 8 10 9 7 5 3 1
ISBN 978-1-78197-594-7

Printed and manufactured in China

SOX

Contents

Northern and Western Europe

Southern and Eastern Europe

Africa

West, Central and South Asia

East and Southeast Asia

Australasia and Oceania

The Poles

Index

Interactive Instructions

On your mobile, or tablet device, download the **FREE** Layar App.

Look out for the **SCAN ME** logo and scan the whole page.

Unlock, discover and enjoy the enhanced content.

For more details, visit: **www.igloobooks.com**

layar

How Earth Was Made

Earth is the planet on which we live. It orbits (travels around) the sun, along with seven other planets, and is itself orbited by the Moon.

Our solar system formed about 4.6 billion years ago, from a vast, swirling mass of dust and gas. Over millions of years the matter clumped together to form the sun and the planets. The sun formed first, followed by the planets, with the nearest one to the sun forming first, then the next, and so on.

The dust and gas from which the solar system formed came from the explosion of a massive star (a supernova). As it exploded with a tremendous bang, it pushed out cool gas (shown here in red).

FASCINATING FACT

Earth is racing through space as it orbits the sun at a speed of about 67,062 mph (107,300 km/h) – that's 1,000 times faster than the speed we drive at on a highway!

The order of the planets from the sun are: Mercury, Venus, Earth, Mars, Jupiter, Saturn, Uranus, Neptune. Between Mars and Jupiter there are thousands of small, rocky asteroids instead of a planet. Out beyond Neptune are a vast number of smaller objects, made of rock, ice or gas, orbiting the sun.

Data Bank

Earth's circumference
24,900 miles (40,075 km)

Earth's surface area
196,939,900 square miles (510,072,000 sq km)

Age of Earth
4,567,200,000 years

Surface temperature (average)
15°C (59°F)

DID YOU KNOW?

Earth's climate and seasons are governed by the sun, which gives off vast amounts of energy. Lands nearer the Equator are warmer, because the sun is directly overhead. At the Poles, the sun's rays have farther to travel through the atmosphere, so the polar climates are colder. The seasons change as Earth shows different sides to the sun during its orbit.

Structure of the Earth

When Earth first formed, it was a mass of molten rock. As the surface cooled, it formed a hard crust around the molten rock, or mantle.

The crust is divided up into a number of gigantic plates that are slowly moving.

AMAZING!

At the center of the Earth is a solid core about 745 miles (1,200 km) deep. It is made up of iron and nickel, and is extremely hot – probably about 6,000°C (10,800°F), which is as hot as the surface of the sun.

DID YOU KNOW?

Earth's slowly moving plates are called tectonic plates. There are nine large plates and a few smaller ones. These plates float on the mantle. They move at less than 1 cm (0.4 in.) a year. Where the plates collide, earthquakes and volcanoes occur.

Around Earth's solid inner core is the outer core, which is about 1,430 miles (2,300 km) thick. This is a thick, slow-moving liquid of iron and nickel. Next comes the 1,800 mile (2,900 km) thick mantle made of molten rock. It gets thicker and more slow-moving the deeper you go. In some places, the mantle bursts out of Earth's crust, through volcanoes.

The Himalayas were, and still are being, formed by the tectonic plate of India colliding with the Asian plate. They are the tallest mountains on Earth.

HAWAII

AMAZING!

The Hawaiian islands were formed at a volcanic hotspot. Molten rock (magma) rises from deep within the mantle to the surface and erupts as lava from Hawaii's five active volcanoes.

Life on Earth

The history of Earth has been divided into a number of periods, each with its own type of rocks and unique forms of life.

The oldest period is known as the Archean Eon. It began about 4,000 million years ago. The rocks from this time were almost all volcanic, and bacteria and other single-celled life forms appeared. From about 650 million years ago, the first forms of life with more than one cell appeared.

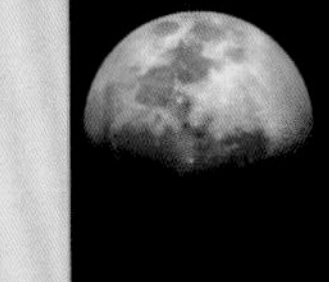

About 300 million years ago, there was just one super-continent, known as Pangaea. It covered almost one-third of the Earth's surface. Pangaea began to break apart about 200 million years ago. It formed two new continents, Gondwana and Laurasia. This changed the climate, making it wetter and warmer.

DID YOU KNOW?

About 230 million years ago the first dinosaurs evolved. They were bigger and more successful than any other land animal at that time. From 70 to 65 million years ago, the huge, fierce meat-eater, *Tyrannosaurus*, roamed the land.

FASCINATING FACTS

- *Tyrannosaurus* had teeth more than 30 cm (12 in.) long – the longest tooth of any hunter ever.
- About 65 million years ago, nearly all life on Earth was wiped out. Scientists think this may have happened when a meteorite hit Earth.

Scientists look at fossils and rocks to find clues about the amazing life that existed on Earth millions of years ago. From fossils they can work out how big a dinosaur was, what it ate, what it looked like and even how it might have behaved.

Between 541 and 252 million years ago, during the Paleozoic Era, plants and animals able to live on land first developed. Great forests of primitive plants sprang up, and invertebrates, amphibians and reptiles evolved. The first modern plants (conifers) also appeared.

Huge sheets of ice have covered the land several times during Earth's history. These periods are known as "ice ages." Animals had to adapt to the new conditions. Successful ice age creatures included woolly mammoths and woolly rhinoceroses.

Woolly mammoths

Earth's Atmosphere

The solid Earth is surrounded by an atmosphere of gasses. These gasses form Earth's weather patterns of wind, rain and varying temperatures.

The atmosphere extends upward for about 75 miles (120 km). About 75% of all the gas in the atmosphere is within 7 miles (11 km) of Earth's surface. The atmosphere is divided into a number of layers, each with its own characteristics.

RAYS FROM SUN

Ultraviolet light from the sun is mostly blocked by the ozone layer. If it wasn't blocked, life on Earth would be impossible. It is ultraviolet light that gives us sunburn.

AMAZING!

Weather balloons are used to carry instruments up into the atmosphere. These send back data about wind speed, temperature, humidity and atmospheric pressure.

The layer of the atmosphere closest to Earth's surface is the troposphere. It is here that weather takes place. Next comes the stratosphere, where ozone gas blocks about 98% of ultraviolet light coming from the sun. The mesosphere is the next layer. The top of the mesosphere is about -100°C (-148°F) and is the coldest part of the atmosphere. Above this is the thermosphere. Many artificial satellites orbit Earth in this layer, on the border between the atmosphere and space. Somewhere about 300 miles (500 km) above Earth's surface, the thermosphere merges with the exosphere.

Because Earth spins, the air closest to the surface gets dragged around as well. Near the Equator, winds tend to blow from east to west, while closer to the Poles they usually blow from west to east.

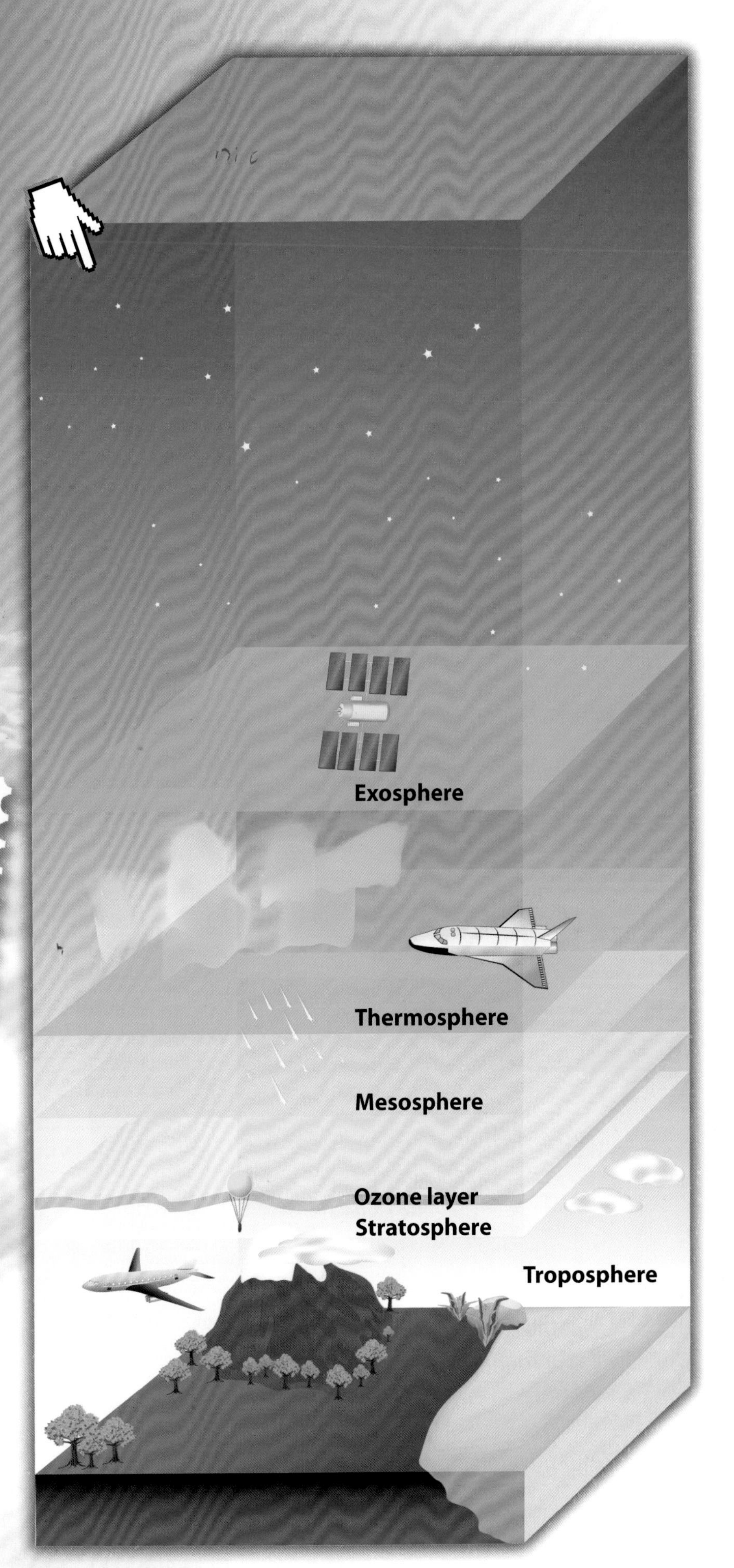

The Oceans

AMAZING!

How are oceans and seas different? An ocean surrounds continents, while seas are surrounded by land.

About 72% of Earth's surface is covered by oceans and seas. The water is salty because over millions of years, minerals from rocks have dissolved into the water.

The depth of the ocean varies enormously from a few meters to several kilometers, depending on the shape of the rocks on the seabed. Continental rocks form a fairly flat area, known as a continental shelf. Waters here are rarely more than about 150 m (490 ft) deep. Sand, mud and silt washed down by rivers ends up on the continental shelf.

FROZEN IN

Part of the Arctic Ocean is so cold that the surface stays frozen all year round. The frozen area increases in winter and recedes in the summer. Global warming is increasing the amount that melts.

Data Bank

Surface areas:

Pacific Ocean
63.8 million square miles
(165 million sq km)

Atlantic Ocean
41.1 million square miles
(106.4 million sq km)

Indian Ocean
28.3 million square miles
(73.5 million sq km)

Arctic Ocean
Atlantic Ocean
Pacific Ocean
Indian Ocean
Southern Ocean

Five oceans cover the planet (the Southern Ocean was only recognized in the year 2000). Most of the ocean floor lies on the ocean crust, and is between 4,000 m (13,100 ft) to 6,000 m (19,685 ft) deep.

AMAZING!

Black smokers are hydrothermal (hot water) vents – chimney-like structures on the ocean floor that emit plumes of hot water and sulfur-bearing minerals that come from beneath Earth's crust.

The manned submersible *Trieste* dived to the deepest part of the world's oceans, the Marianas Trench, in 1960. The deepest point is nearly 6.8 miles (11 km) below the surface. In 2012, James Cameron made the first solo dive to the Marianas Trench.

North America

North America stretches from the Arctic Ocean to Central America. Mountain ranges run down the east and west sides, and between them lies a vast area of almost flat land. In the north the climate is very cold, while in the south it is much warmer.

The first humans to live in North America arrived from Asia about 25,000 years ago. They walked there via a land bridge that used to exist between Alaska (above) and Asia.

VISAS 11

Stats and Facts

Countries:
United States of America, Canada

Largest City:
New York, 18.9 million people

Tallest Mountain:
Mount McKinley in Alaska, USA, 6,194 m (20,320 ft)

Longest River:
The Missouri–Mississippi river system, USA, at 3,900 miles (6,300 km) long

Meaning of name:
From Amerigo Vespucci, the Italian cartographer who produced early maps of the Americas.

HAWAII

AMAZING!

Of the United States' 50 states, 48 are adjoining, but the island state of Hawaii lies far out in the Pacific Ocean. To the north, the huge state of Alaska is separated from the rest of the country by part of Canada.

Hudson Bay is an area of shallow sea almost entirely surrounded by North America. It covers 475,000 square miles (1,230,000 sq km) and is about 100 m (328 ft) deep.
The island of Newfoundland is part of the Canadian province of Newfoundland and Labrador. It was visited by the Italian explorer John Cabot, working under contract to King Henry VII of England, on his expedition from Bristol in 1497.
The Rocky Mountains extend for 3,000 miles (4,830 km) from north to south.
FASCINATING FACTS
Mexico is geographically part of North America, but culturally and politically it forms part of Central America.
Much of the border between the United States and Mexico is formed by the Rio Grande, which empties via a sandy delta into the Gulf of Mexico.
SCAN ME
Instructions on page 5
CANADA
Hudson Bay
NORTHWEST TERRITORIES
BRITISH COLUMBIA
ALBERTA
SASKATCHEWAN
MANITOBA
ONTARIO
QUEBEC
NEWFOUNDLAND & LABRADOR
PRINCE EDWARD IS.
NEW BRUNSWICK
NOVA SCOTIA
Inuvik
Ft. Norman
Mackenzie
Yellowknife
Rankin Inlet
Churchill
Goose Bay
St. John's
Edmonton
Calgary
Saskatoon
Regina
Winnipeg
Vancouver
Moosonee
Thunder Bay
Halifax
Montreal
Ottawa
Toronto
Peace
Athabasca
N. Saskatchewan
S. Saskatchewan
St. Lawrence
ROCKY MOUNTAINS
Missouri
Lake Superior
Lake Michigan
Lake Huron
Lake Erie
Lake Ontario
Mississippi
Red
Colorado
Rio Grande
Alabama
WASHINGTON
OREGON
IDAHO
MONTANA
NORTH DAKOTA
MINNESOTA
WISCONSIN
MICHIGAN
NEVADA
IOWA
ILLINOIS
INDIANA
OHIO
PENNSYLVANIA
NEW YORK
VERMONT
MAINE
NEW HAMPSHIRE
MASSACHUSETTS
RHODE ISLAND
CONNECTICUT
NEW JERSEY
DELAWARE
MARYLAND
WASHINGTON D.C.
WEST VIRGINIA
VIRGINIA
KENTUCKY
TENNESSEE
NORTH CAROLINA
SOUTH CAROLINA
GEORGIA
ALABAMA
MISSISSIPPI
LOUISIANA
ARKANSAS
MISSOURI
KANSAS
NEW MEXICO
TEXAS
Seattle
Olympia
Helena
Bismarck
St. Paul
Boise
Pierre
Madison
Lansing
Detroit
Chicago
Des Moines
Lincoln
Carson City
Las Vegas
Los Angeles
San Diego
Phoenix
Topeka
Jefferson City
St. Louis
Springfield
Indianapolis
Columbus
Frankfort
Charleston
Richmond
Harrisburg
Annapolis
Dover
Trenton
New York City
Hartford
Providence
Boston
Albany
Concord
Montpelier
Augusta
Nashville
Raleigh
Columbia
Atlanta
Savannah
Montgomery
Tallahassee
Jackson
Little Rock
Oklahoma City
Dallas
Austin
San Antonio
Houston
Baton Rouge
New Orleans
El Paso
ATLANTIC OCEAN
BERMUDA
MEXICO
Hermosillo
Chihuahua
Monterrey
Tampico
Mérida
Leon
Guadalajara
Mexico City
Acapulco

Habitats and Wildlife

North America has a wide variety of natural habitats due to its great size and varied geography.

The far north is covered by tundra – a treeless area covered in grass and lichen. The winters are so long and cold that no other plants can grow there. During the short summers, the plants grow quickly, attracting lots of animals. Huge herds of caribou move north each spring, then return south in the fall. Wolves move alongside the caribou herds, preying on weak or old animals. Geese and other birds fly in to feast on the summer plants. They lay their eggs there and raise their young, before flying south for the winter.

The cougar is the biggest wild cat in North America. It stands 90 cm (35 in.) tall at the shoulder and may be up to 2.4 m (8 ft) long. The cougar is thriving thanks to its broad range of prey, which includes deer, goats, sheep and rabbits.

AMAZING!

Wetlands – swamps, marshes and bayous – cover large areas of southeastern North America. Many waterbirds, reptiles and mammals live in the Everglades, including alligators.

AMAZING!

Wolves were once common throughout all of North America, but by the mid 1930s hunting had greatly reduced their range. Now they are mainly found in Alaska, Canada and some northern US states.

Grizzly bears feed on grass, berries, fish and small mammals. They rarely hunt humans, but can be aggressive if they feel threatened. One or two people – usually hikers or campers – are killed by grizzlies each year.

FASCINATING FACTS

- Some people have reported seeing a large ape living in the forests of northwestern North America. This creature is called Bigfoot, or Sasquatch.
- Bigfoot is said to be up to 2.5 m (8 ft) tall and to walk upright like a human.
- Many people claim to have seen Bigfoot, but nobody has proved it really exists.

Peoples

The first people to live in North America came from Asia more than 15,000 years ago. They were the ancestors of today's Inuit and Native Americans. Then, from the late 15th century, other people came from Europe, Africa and Asia.

Before the arrival of European settlers, Native Americans lived throughout the region in separate tribes, each with its own language, culture and territory. Millions died from introduced diseases and in clashes with the settlers. Their number fell from 12 million in 1400 to 250,000 in 1900. Today, about 3.2 million descendants of Native Americans live in North America.

AMAZING!

The biggest Native American tribe today is the Cherokee, with a population of 281,000. The smallest tribe is the Augustine Cahuilla, with a population of 8.

The Inuit of the Arctic traditionally lived by hunting seals, fishing and making clothes from seal and caribou hides. Many Inuit now have regular jobs, but they remain proud of their traditions.

AMAZING!

Vikings from Europe
Europeans first arrived in North America about the year 1000, when an Icelander named Leif Ericson landed in Newfoundland. The Icelanders came to cut timber for use on Greenland. They continued to visit to cut timber until about 1350.

Data Bank

North American population

African-Americans
about 12%

Asian or Asian descent
about 5%

Central or South American
about 9%

DID YOU KNOW?

Europeans first settled in North America during the 16th century. Africans began arriving in the 17th century, brought over as slaves by European settlers. In recent years, many immigrants have come from Asia.

The Spanish explored southwestern North America in the 1500s, and in 1521 conquered the Aztecs of Mexico. More than 22 million Hispanic Americans now live in the United States.

Canada

The northern part of North America is occupied by the country of Canada.

Canada was formed in 1867, when a number of colonies within the British Empire came together to become a new country. Canada is now made up of 10 provinces and three territories, all under the authority of a central government based in the city of Ottawa.

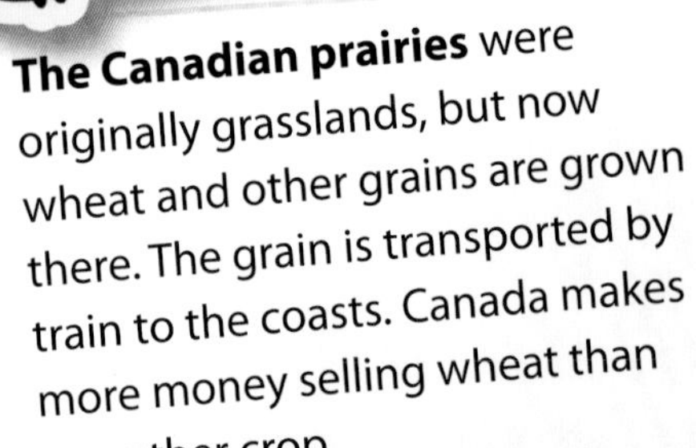

The Canadian prairies were originally grasslands, but now wheat and other grains are grown there. The grain is transported by train to the coasts. Canada makes more money selling wheat than any other crop.

At the town of Calgary, cowboys used to gather to compete in games based on their horsemanship skills. The first contests were held in 1886. In 1912 the event was named the Calgary Stampede. Today, the Stampede lasts for 10 days and attracts 1.2 million visitors.

DID YOU KNOW?

Massive explosion
In 1917, in Halifax, Nova Scotia, the SS *Mont Blanc* caught fire while carrying a full load of explosives. The blast flattened hundreds of buildings and damaged 12,000 more. Some 2,000 people were killed and 9,000 injured.

QUEBEC

Data Bank

Area:
9,984,000 sq km

Population:
33,476,000

Product per person:
$41,506

AMAZING!

Quebec was originally a French colony. It was captured by the British in 1763, but the French settlers stayed in Quebec and most people in the area speak French. The capital of Quebec is Quebec City, with a population of 516,000.

The CN Tower is a famous landmark in the city of Toronto. It stands 553 m (1,814 ft) tall and was completed in 1976. When it was built, it was the tallest building in the world. The tower is used to broadcast telecommunications signals across the flat Canadian prairies.

The Inuit are the descendants of the people who lived in Canada before European settlers arrived. Although the far north is their homeland, over the past 50 years many have moved south to get jobs in factories and offices.

Western USA

The western third of North America is covered by the Western Cordillera. This vast range of mountains, plateaux and basins extends from Alaska to Mexico.

There are three main belts of mountains within the cordillera: the Pacific Coast Ranges in the west, the Sierra Nevada in the center, and the Laramide belt in the east, which includes the Rocky Mountains.

Pueblo houses were traditionally built by the indigenous Zuni, Hopi and Laguna tribes, who live in the south. The houses are made of mud, stones and timber, and cluster around a central town plaza.

AMAZING!

San Francisco stands on a large bay on the Pacific Coast. Its most famous feature is the Golden Gate Bridge, which crosses the entrance to the bay. Some 20% of the city's 7.6 million people originate from China.

FASCINATING FACTS

- The Grand Canyon is a vast, steep-sided valley that has been carved by the Colorado River over the last 15 million years.
- The Canyon is 277 miles (446 km) long, 18 miles (29 km) wide and 1.1 mile (1.8 km) deep.
- The majestic scenery of the Canyon attracts 5 million visitors each year.

Hollywood Boulevard runs through Hollywood in southern California. This town has been the heart of the American movie industry since 1906. By 1920, more movies were being made here than anywhere else in the world. Movies are still made here.

DID YOU KNOW?

This redwood tree, named General Sherman, is the largest tree in the world. Redwood trees, or sequoia, grow on the slopes of the Western Cordillera. Two species are native to this area and were once found nowhere else, but today they can be seen in gardens and parks around the world.

Midwest USA

The Midwest is the northern central area of the United States. It includes the states of Illinois, Indiana, Iowa, Kansas, Michigan, Minnesota, Missouri, Nebraska, North Dakota, Ohio, South Dakota and Wisconsin.

The area is rich in agricultural lands and industry. The east is hilly with higher rainfall. To the north lie the Great Lakes. Further west the land is flatter and drier, and was originally prairie grassland grazed by bison.

Gangsters

Chicago was formerly famous for organized crime bosses, such as Al Capone, Jim Colosimo and George Moran. In one notorious incident on 14 February, 1929, the Capone Gang murdered seven members of the Moran Gang.

DID YOU KNOW?

Blueberries are well suited to the northern regions of the Midwest, which have a cooler, damper climate. Other fruits grown include cherries, apples, grapes, peaches, plums, pears and strawberries.

The city of Chicago is a major port on the Great Lakes. It has a population of 2.7 million, making it the third-largest city in the USA. The city has a varied economy that includes factories, banking and service industries.

Mount Rushmore in South Dakota depicts four US presidents – Washington, Jefferson, Lincoln and Theodore Roosevelt.

DID YOU KNOW?

Politics is important in the Midwest. Because the population is representative of the whole country, politicians like to try out ideas here. The Iowa Caucus takes place every four years at the start of the electoral process to choose a new president. Thousands of journalists pour into Iowa to watch the event.

Southern States USA

The southern states cover the southeastern part of the USA. They comprise Florida, Georgia, Maryland, North Carolina, South Carolina, Virginia, West Virginia, Delaware, Alabama, Kentucky, Mississippi, Tennessee, Arkansas, Louisiana, Oklahoma and Texas.

The Florida Everglades are hot in the summer, cool in the winter and wet all year round. The biggest wetland animal is the alligator, which can grow up to 4.4 m (14 ft) long and is known to live for up to 75 years!

AMAZING!

Cape Canaveral in Florida is the largest spaceport in North America. The site was chosen partly because of the usually clear weather and the fact that launches could be sent over the ocean, so if anything went wrong, debris would fall into the sea.

AMERICAN QUEEN
NEW ORLEANS, LA.

AMAZING!

New Orleans is famous for jazz. It is also a major port. Ships from around the world dock here to transfer goods to Mississippi barges, trains and trucks. In recent years, large oil deposits have been found offshore, and the oil industry is thriving.

In 1861, 11 of the southern states left the United States of America to form the Confederate States of America. The US government declared this was not allowed, and a war began. The Civil War lasted four years and caused about 1 million deaths. The economy of the South has never properly recovered.

The Mississippi River drains 1.1 million square miles (2.9 million sq km) of North America. At its mouth, mud and sand brought down by the river form a vast delta of swamps. The 1830s was the golden age of steamboats on the river. They were used to transport cotton, rice, timber, tobacco and molasses.

New England USA

New England is the name given to the northeastern states. It was the first area to be settled by the English during the 17th century.

The culture of the area is strongly influenced by its British heritage. However, this was also the area that led the way in seeking independence from Britain.

Boston, Massachusetts, was founded in 1630 by settlers from England. It now has a population of 630,000 and is a major center for banking and financial services. The colleges and universities in and around the city attract large numbers of students and help boost the economy.

The Liberty Bell, in Pennsylvania, Philadelphia, was rung to summon people to listen to the Declaration of Independence being read in public for the first time. Independence from Britain was voted for on 4 July, 1776.

FASCINATING FACTS

- The smallest state in the USA is Rhode Island, which has an area of 1,212 square miles (3,140 sq km).
- Although Rhode Island has a population of just 1 million, it elects 2 senators to the US Congress – the same as all the other states.

RED SOX

AMAZING!

Dreadful disaster

On 4 July, 1866, a firework set fire to a pile of wood in Portland, Maine. The fire spread rapidly and by the time it was put out it had destroyed 1,800 buildings.

The Boston Red Sox baseball team is one of the most famous in the world. It was founded in 1901 and has won seven World Series titles. The team is famous for the red socks worn by the players. The Red Sox have a famous rivalry with the Yankees from New York.

The Cape Cod peninsula sticks out from the coast of Massachusetts into the Atlantic Ocean. The warm summer weather and long, sandy beaches have made it a popular holiday resort. Many visitors go whale watching, or attend the music festival in August.

The forests of New England are mostly composed of deciduous trees, such as maple, birch, beech, elm and ash. In the fall, the leaves turn red, orange, yellow and brown, and are breathtakingly beautiful. Visitors come in huge numbers to see them, especially on the rolling, tree-covered hills of Vermont.

Central and South America

Central America is the long peninsula extending from the southern USA to Colombia, plus the islands of the Caribbean. South America stretches from just north of the Equator almost to Antarctica.

Central and South America are joined by a narrow strip of land called the Isthmus of Panama.

Machu Picchu is a 15th-century Inca site, re-discovered in 1911 by the American archeologist Hiram Bingham. He found the entire town in almost perfect condition – only the wooden roofs were missing.

MACHU PICCHU

VISAS 11

Stats and Facts

Central America countries:
Belize, Costa Rica, El Salvador, Guatemala, Honduras, Mexico, Nicaragua, Panama.
Largest City: Mexico City, 8.8 million people

Caribbean countries:
Antigua & Barbuda, Bahamas, Barbados, Cuba, Dominica, Dominican Republic, Grenada, Haiti, Jamaica, Saint Kitts & Nevis, Saint Lucia, Saint Vincent & the Grenadines and Trinidad & Tobago.

South America countries:
Argentina, Bolivia, Brazil, Chile, Colombia, Ecuador, Guyana, Paraguay, Peru, Suriname, Uruguay and Venezuela.
Largest City: São Paulo, 11.3 million people

DID YOU KNOW?

Lake Titicaca lies on the border of Peru and Bolivia. At 3,812 m (12,507 ft) above sea level, it is the highest large lake in the world. The lake's floating islands made of reeds are a tourist attraction.

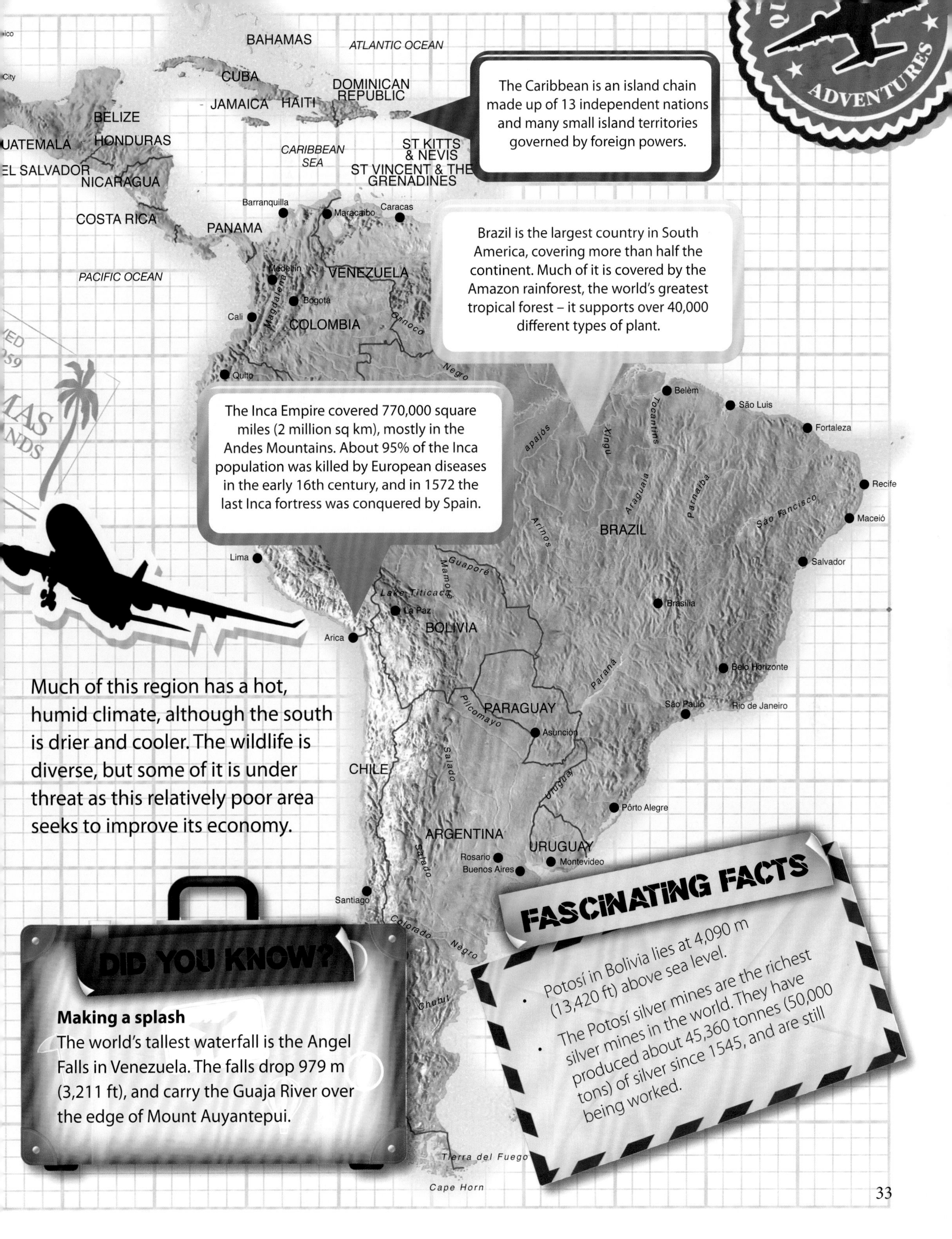

The Caribbean is an island chain made up of 13 independent nations and many small island territories governed by foreign powers.

Brazil is the largest country in South America, covering more than half the continent. Much of it is covered by the Amazon rainforest, the world's greatest tropical forest – it supports over 40,000 different types of plant.

The Inca Empire covered 770,000 square miles (2 million sq km), mostly in the Andes Mountains. About 95% of the Inca population was killed by European diseases in the early 16th century, and in 1572 the last Inca fortress was conquered by Spain.

Much of this region has a hot, humid climate, although the south is drier and cooler. The wildlife is diverse, but some of it is under threat as this relatively poor area seeks to improve its economy.

DID YOU KNOW?

Making a splash

The world's tallest waterfall is the Angel Falls in Venezuela. The falls drop 979 m (3,211 ft), and carry the Guaja River over the edge of Mount Auyantepui.

FASCINATING FACTS

- Potosí in Bolivia lies at 4,090 m (13,420 ft) above sea level.
- The Potosí silver mines are the richest silver mines in the world. They have produced about 45,360 tonnes (50,000 tons) of silver since 1545, and are still being worked.

Habitats and Wildlife

As well as rainforest in the wettest areas, the region also has mountains, deserts in the driest areas and grasslands in the moderately wet areas. Different habitats support different types of wildlife.

The Sonoran Desert covers part of northern Mexico and the southern United States. It is home to numerous animals and plants adapted to the hot, dry climate – for example the saguaro cactus, which it is illegal to cut down.

DID YOU KNOW?

Armadillos live in Central and South America, particularly in Paraguay, where they dig for grubs. They are the only mammal to have armor. There are about 20 species, some now very rare.

MANATEE

AMAZING

The manatee is a water mammal that swims around the coasts of Central America and up the Amazon River. It feeds on leaves and other water vegetation, eating its own body weight in food every 10 days.

HARPY EAGLE

FASCINATING FACTS

- Large areas of the pampas grasslands of southeastern South America are now used to graze cattle or grow crops.
- Animals of the pampas grasslands include the pampas deer, pampas fox and the rhea – a giant, flightless bird up to 1.8 m (6 ft) tall.

Opossums are small marsupials (mammals whose young develop in pouches). There are more than 100 species. Opossums feed on fruit, leaves, birds, amphibians and snakes – most are immune to snake venom.

The harpy eagle is the largest and most powerful bird of prey in the Americas. It has a wingspan of up to 2.3 m (7.5 ft). This eagle hunts monkeys, sloths and other forest animals, and can lift an animal as heavy as itself.

DID YOU KNOW?

Coyotes are wild dogs that range across Central and North America. These medium-sized dogs hunt mice, squirrels, lizards and birds, and will sometimes eat fruits and shoots.

Peoples

Some of the people who live in South and Central America are descendents of the original inhabitants who migrated from Asia over 12,000 years ago. Others are descendents of the European settlers, and some have mixed ancestry. There are many more Native Americans in Central and South America than in North America.

DID YOU KNOW?

Central American cooking is a blend of local ingredients and styles imported from Spain. Corn, beans and chili peppers are combined to make distinctive dishes, such as tacos, chili con carne and tortilla (above).

AMAZING!

Carnival celebrations are held in towns and villages throughout South America before the start of Lent, usually in February. Much the biggest and most spectacular is the four-day Rio Carnival, held in Rio de Janeiro, Brazil.

The Mestizo are the largest population group in Central and South America. They are descended from indigenous Americans and Spanish settlers.

Data Bank

Five biggest cities:

São Paulo
20 million

Buenos Aires
13.6 million

Rio de Janeiro
12 million

Lima
9.1 million

Mexico City
8.8 million

BRAZIL

People with an unmixed Spanish or Portuguese ancestry generally see themselves as separate from other peoples living in the region. They are known as Criollo, or Crioulu in Brazil.

MAYANS

DID YOU KNOW?

The Maya people live across a large area of Central America. There are about 6 million, living mostly in rural areas. The Maya proudly preserve their culture and traditions.

Mexico

Mexico is the largest country in Central America. It became independent of Spain in 1821, then lost its northern territories to the USA in a series of wars. After many years of poverty and upheaval, Mexico now has a stable government and is increasingly wealthy.

Data Bank

Population
115,297,000

Area
761,586 square miles
(1,972,500 sq km)

Government
Federal Republic

Currency
Mexican Peso

Product per person
$15,300

The largest city in Mexico is the capital, Mexico City, with a population of nearly 9 million. During the later 20th century the city grew to be a major industrial city with important banking and administrative industries.

DID YOU KNOW?

The Day of the Dead festival takes place every year on 1st and 2nd November. It is a time when people remember their friends and relatives who have died. The festival is a happy occasion and an excuse for parties.

DID YOU KNOW?

Mastretta is a Mexican car company founded in 1987. Since 2010 it has been making the MXT – the first sports car to be manufactured in large numbers in Central or South America.

MARIACHI BAND

MADE IN MEXICO

Mariachi is a traditional form of folk music from western Mexico, played by a large band on stringed instruments. Some bands include trumpets, too. The singers wear colorful clothes, and the men may wear sombreros – the traditional wide-brimmed Mexican hat.

AMAZING!

The stock exchange in Mexico City is the largest in Central America. Shares in companies from across the region are traded there. The total value of shares in this exchange in 2012 was $460 billion.

STOCK EXCHANGE

Guatemala,

Belize, El Salvador, Honduras, Nicaragua, Panama and Costa Rica

The southern part of Central America is mountainous with fertile valleys suitable for farming. The climate is hot and damp. The area has seen frequent wars and revolutions, but since the 1980s the political systems have become more stable and the economy has improved.

TIKAL RUINS

The ruined cities of Copan and Tikal were built by the Mayans more than 1500 years ago. The temples tower up to 50 m (165 ft) tall. Originally these would have been surrounded by wooden houses for up to 100,000 people. The cities were abandoned about AD 900. Today they are major tourist attractions.

FASCINATING FACTS

- Nicaragua is home to five species of wild cat: the jaguar, cougar, jaguarundi, margay and ocelot.
- Lake Nicaragua is the only large lake in the world that is home to a species of shark – the Nicaraguan bull shark.

Managua is the capital of Nicaragua. The city is a busy trading center for coffee and cotton. It enjoys a beautiful setting on the shores of Lake Xolotlán (or Lake Managua).

AMAZING!

Palm oil is one of the most profitable crops in the region. Traditionally it was used in local cooking, but since the 1990s it has also been used to make diesel fuel for motor vehicles.

DID YOU KNOW?

Dance crazy

The Mestizaje dance, from the Pacific Coast, is performed by a couple and tells the story of a romance. As part of the dance, the man seeks to impress his colorfully dressed partner with his elegant dance moves.

PANAMA CITY PANAMA ARRIVED MAR. 1959

The Panama Canal was completed in 1914. It carries ocean-going ships to and fro between the Pacific and Atlantic oceans across Central America. When it first opened, it carried about 1,000 ships a year; now it carries about 15,000.

PANAMA CANAL

DID YOU KNOW?

The red-eyed tree frog lives only in the rainforests of Central America. It clambers among the branches at night looking for insects to eat, and comes down to the ground to lay its eggs in ponds or puddles.

Caribbean

A chain of about 700 islands extends across the Caribbean Sea from Florida in the north to South America in the south.

Tourism is a major employer in the Caribbean. About 12 million visitors fly to the islands each year to enjoy the warm weather and sandy beaches. Another 7 million visit on board cruise ships. Scuba diving on the coral reefs is a popular tourist activity.

ARRIVED MAR. 1959 JAMAICA ... BAY

AMAZING!

The hurricane season lasts from July to October. About six hurricanes form each year. These massively powerful storms can devastate communities, wrecking homes and killing thousands.

HURRICANE DAMAGE

DID YOU KNOW?

Jerk chicken is a famous Caribbean dish from Jamaica. The chicken is rubbed all over with a mix of herbs and spices, and is grilled or roasted over a fire.

Data Bank

Land Area
92,548 square miles (239,700 sq km)

Population
39,170,000

The larger islands to the north are known as the Greater Antilles, and the smaller islands to the east are the Lesser Antilles.

Spanish settlers brought banana plants to the Caribbean from Asia in the 1530s. They were well-suited to the hot, wet climate, and became an important export crop. Today, however, competition from India and Africa has reduced the banana trade.

The voodoo religion developed from about 1730, when slaves brought to the Caribbean from Africa started mixing their beliefs with the Christian religion of the slave owners.

FASCINATING FACTS

- Sugarcane was brought to the Caribbean by Spanish settlers in the 1490s. By the 1700s it was the main crop of the islands.
- Sugarcane was grown on plantations worked by slaves. The landowners made huge profits.

South America

The continent of South America stretches from just north of the Equator almost to Antarctica. The bulk of the land area lies within the tropics, with a narrow tail stretching south into cooler climates.

The landscape is dominated by two vast regions. In the west, the Andes Mountains run the full length of the continent. To the east lie flat lands dominated by river basins and mostly covered by dense rainforest. People live mostly around the coast, with only small populations in the interior.

Data Bank

Area
6.9 million square miles (17.8 million sq km)

Population
387,490,000

Countries
Argentina, Bolivia, Brazil, Chile, Colombia, Ecuador, Guyana, Paraguay, Peru, Surinam, Uruguay, Venezuela

DID YOU KNOW?

The mighty Iguazo Falls on the border between Brazil and Argentina are the widest falls in the world and the second-largest in terms of water flow. They stand 75 m (246 ft) tall and spray rises up to 150 m (492 ft) above them.

The Atacama Desert in Chile is the driest place in the world. It covers about 40,540 square miles (105,000 sq km) along the coast, and rainfall averages just 0.01 cm (0.004 in.) a year.

AWESOME FACT!

Aconcagua is the highest mountain in South America, and the highest mountain in the world that can be climbed without ropes, picks or pins. It stands 6,960 m (22,834 ft) tall.

FASCINATING FACTS

- Piranha fish live in rivers, lakes and streams in South America.
- The fish swim in large shoals and can kill creatures much larger than themselves.

ACONCAGUA

Football is a passion in South America, especially in Brazil. Brazil has won the Soccer World Cup five times – more than any other country.

DID YOU KNOW?

The Andes

The Andes extend 4,350 miles (7,000 km) north to south. The chain is made up of several ranges separated by high plateaux and low basins. There are large deposits of copper, tin, silver and gold in the mountains, as well as oil and gas.

Northern and Western Europe

The continent of Europe is a vast peninsula pushing out from the west of Asia. This region has a long and rugged coastline, and many islands.

The biggest islands are Iceland, Great Britain and Ireland. From the mainland, the Danish, Scandinavian and Breton peninsulas push out into the sea. Culturally the area is dominated by peoples speaking Germanic or Celtic languages. The countries include some of the wealthiest, most industrialized and most densely populated on Earth.

Monaco is a tiny state on the Mediterranean coast, and is the most densely populated country in the world. It has an amazing 45,781 people per square mile (17,675 people per sq km)!

VISAS 11

Stats and Facts

Countries:
Iceland, Norway, Sweden, Finland, Denmark, Latvia, Lithuania, Estonia, United Kingdom, Ireland, France, Monaco, Andorra, Luxembourg, Belgium, The Netherlands, Liechtenstein, Germany, Austria, Switzerland.

Largest City:
London 8.1 million people

Tallest Mountain:
Mont Blanc, on the French/Italian/Swiss border, 4,807 m (15,771 ft).

Longest River:
The Rhine, 1,390 km (865 mi.)

Iceland is a volcanic island. It was formed by volcanoes erupting along the crack in the Earth's crust between the European and North American tectonic plates. Hot springs bubble up all over the island, some perfect for bathing in!

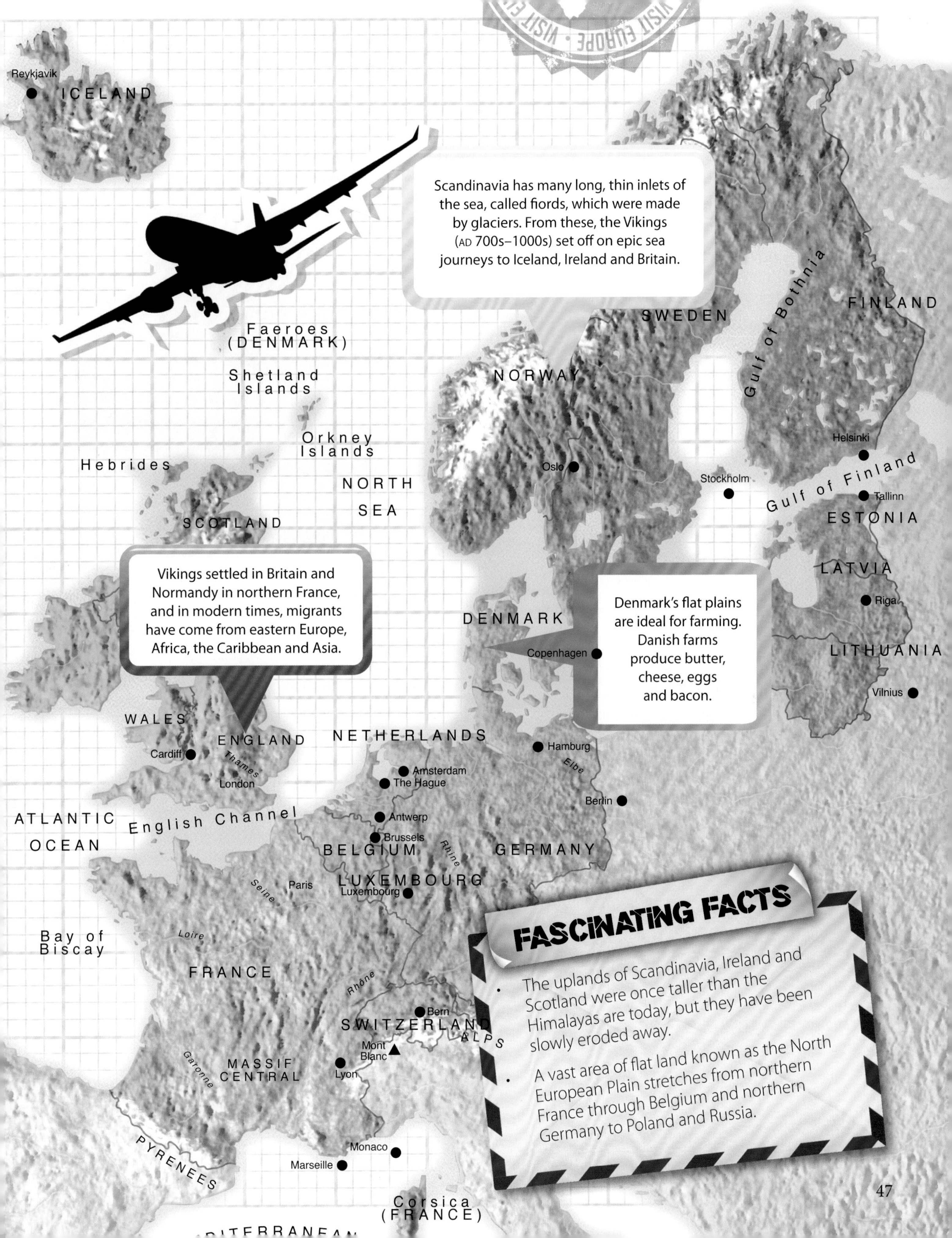

Scandinavia has many long, thin inlets of the sea, called fiords, which were made by glaciers. From these, the Vikings (AD 700s–1000s) set off on epic sea journeys to Iceland, Ireland and Britain.

Vikings settled in Britain and Normandy in northern France, and in modern times, migrants have come from eastern Europe, Africa, the Caribbean and Asia.

Denmark's flat plains are ideal for farming. Danish farms produce butter, cheese, eggs and bacon.

FASCINATING FACTS

- The uplands of Scandinavia, Ireland and Scotland were once taller than the Himalayas are today, but they have been slowly eroded away.
- A vast area of flat land known as the North European Plain stretches from northern France through Belgium and northern Germany to Poland and Russia.

Habitats and Wildlife

Most of northern and western Europe was originally covered by vast tracts of forest.

In the north, these remain largely intact, as the soils are too poor for farming and the area is not heavily settled by humans. The trees are evergreen, and the forest is known as boreal forest. Farther south, deciduous trees such as oak, ash, elm and birch once covered the land. The southern forests have mostly been felled to make way for farms, towns and cities.

GOLDFINCH

Goldfinches live in loose colonies anywhere where there are scattered bushes and trees. They use their beaks to extract seeds from thistles and teasels. In winter, many migrate as far south as southern Spain.

AMAZING!

Brown bears once lived across most of northern Eurasia, but overhunting means they are now rare. There is a tiny population in the Pyrenees, and larger numbers in Italy, Sweden, Finland, Estonia and Norway.

Happy Journey

AMAZING!

Boreal forest

A belt of boreal (or taiga) forest extends right across Europe and Asia to North America. In Europe, the belt crosses Scotland and Scandinavia. The most common trees are firs, spruce, pine and larch.

Oak is a typical tree of the southern forests. Oak trees can grow to be more than 20 m (65 ft) tall and can live for more than 1,000 years. Most of the big oaks in Europe have been cut down and their hard, dense wood used to build houses.

DID YOU KNOW?

Reindeer are an important grazing animal in the far north. They feed on grass, leaves, moss and lichens. This varied diet, combined with thick fur, enables them to survive in cold climates. Herds of reindeer are kept by the Sami and Nenet peoples.

Peoples

Europe saw a wave of immigration in the 5th and 6th centuries, when peoples such as the Huns, Alans and Magyars moved in to Europe from Asia. This caused the peoples of Europe to move and mix.

During the 20th century, another large wave of immigrants came to some parts of Europe from Africa and Asia.

FRENCH MOROCCAN

Immigrants came to France in large numbers from its former colonies in Africa during the years after 1950. Today, 5.3 million people living in France are immigrants, while 6.7 million are the children of immigrants. They mostly live in two areas: Paris and the south coast.

Southern Germany has a distinctive culture based on its traditional occupations of farming, logging and animal herding on the mountains. Traditional music is played on brass instruments and has a rousing, march-like beat.

AMAZING!

The Celts

The Irish belong to a group known as the Celts. Originally the Celts lived across much of Europe, from Ireland to Spain and northern Italy to Romania. Today, Celtic languages and culture survive only in Ireland, Wales, Scotland and Brittany in northern France.

DID YOU KNOW?

Britain has a dynamic, multi-ethnic society. West Indians, Indians and Pakistanis, among others, form an important part of British culture. This is nowhere more apparent than at the Notting Hill Carnival, which has been held every August in London since 1966.

AMAZING!

Scottish Highlanders have their own social and cultural life, originally based around the clan – a tribe of related families. The traditional music of the Highlands is played on the bagpipes. Formal Highland dress is usually worn for special events, such as weddings.

UK and Ireland

The British Isles are the islands that lie off the northwest coast of Europe.

The two largest islands are Ireland and Great Britain, but there are actually dozens of small inhabited islands and thousands of uninhabited islands in the group. The British Isles are two countries: The Republic of Ireland and the United Kingdom of England, Scotland and Northern Ireland. Among the historic peoples of the British Isles are the English, Scots, Welsh, Cornish, Manx, Irish and Orcadians. The English account for about 70% of the people in the British Isles.

The Mini car is an iconic British car. It was first produced in 1959 by the British car company Morris. More than 5 million have since been made. In 2001 the German car company BMW began making a new car styled to look like the famous Mini.

THERE IS NO DARKNESS BUT IGNORANCE

DID YOU KNOW?

William Shakespeare (1564–1616) is the most famous playwright ever to have lived. He was born in Stratford-upon-Avon. His works have been translated into more than 200 languages, and are performed more often than those of any other playwright.

AMAZING!

The Scottish Parliament has 129 members and is elected once every four years. Scotland voted to have its own Parliament in 1997 so that it could make some of its own laws, but it remains part of the United Kingdom. Wales has a similar body called the Welsh Assembly.

AMAZING!

The Rock of Cashel was an important religious center for Ireland from about 440 to 1749. The ruined cathedral, chapel, fortress and tower are now important tourist attractions.

The royal family dates back to a man named Cerdic, who became the ruler of an area of southern England in about AD 490. Today the monarch has little power, but leads the nation in important rituals and celebrations.

Data Bank

Area
121,673 square miles (315,134 sq km)

Population
68,215,000

Number of islands
About 6,000

Highest point
Ben Nevis, 1,344 m (4,409 ft)

France

and the Low Countries

France is a large republic in the southwest of the region. To the northeast lie Belgium, the Netherlands and Luxembourg, which are known as the Low Countries, since most of the terrain is flat and close to sea level.

France is mountainous in the south and the northwest, but elsewhere is generally low lying and covered by fertile farmland.

The Afsluitdijk is a 20 mile (32 km) long dam in the Netherlands that cuts off the huge, shallow bay of Zuiderzee from the North Sea. In all, four large areas have been surrounded by dams and drained, creating 620 square miles (1,600 sq km) of new land.

AMSTERDAM

Amsterdam in the Netherlands was built on wet, low-lying ground. A series of canals were dug to drain away the water and provide a transport network. The canals are crossed by 1,500 bridges and divide the city into 90 islands.

AMAZING!

The Château de Chambord was built by King Francois I of France as a holiday home in the Loire Valley. It has 440 rooms and 82 staircases, and is now a major tourist attraction.

Data Bank

Area
213,043,449 square miles
(551,780,000 sq km)

Population
91 million

Highest Mountain
Mont Blanc, 4,810 m
(15,780 ft)

Longest River
Loire, 629 miles (1,012 km)

TGV

Happy Journey

AMAZING!

The Eiffel Tower was built in Paris in 1889 for the World Fair. The iron tower is 320 m (1,049 ft) tall, and was built to serve as the entrance to the Fair. It was intended to be temporary, but it became so famous that it was preserved. The tower is named after Gustav Eiffel, the engineer who built it. Every year, more than 7 million people go to the top to see the views of Paris.

France's TGV train is a high-speed service that runs on specially built tracks and links the major cities of France. Scheduled services regularly reach 320 km/h (200 mph), but one test train set the record for the fastest wheeled train, reaching 574.8 km/h (357.2 mph) in 2007.

FASCINATING FACTS

- During the 1870s, a group of French artists developed a new style of painting that came to be called Impressionism.
- Instead of painting realistically, the artists conveyed feelings and impressions. This was the start of modern art.

Brussels Euro Parliament
Most countries in Europe belong to the European Union. This organization has its headquarters in Brussels, Belgium. The peoples of Europe elect representatives to go to the European Parliament to supervise the activities of the European Union.

Scandinavia

Scandinavia is the name given to the countries inhabited by the Scandinavian peoples. It comprises Norway, Sweden, Denmark, Iceland and associated territories such as Greenland, the Faroe Islands and Svalbard.

Finland is often grouped with the other Scandinavian countries. However, the Finnish language is linked to Estonian, Hungarian and Karelian, and the Finns share cultural traits with peoples from northwestern Russia. Geographically, the land is more akin to Russia.

Vast oilfields and gasfields were discovered under the North Sea in the 1950s. Oil rigs were built to drill down to the oil and gas, which was sent ashore by pipeline. Oil is still extracted on a large scale, but the reserves are getting harder to reach.

AMAZING!

The Gokstad ship is about 1,000 years old. It was found in a burial mound in Norway. This was the type of ship used by the Vikings when they set sail across the North Atlantic. The ship is 23 m (75 ft) long, and could carry about 70 people.

The Lofoten Islands lie north of the Arctic Circle off the north coast of Norway. Here, at midsummer, the sun never falls below the horizon, and in midwinter it never rises – hence the name, Land of the Midnight Sun.

Data Bank

Area
1,222,013 square miles (3,165,000 sq km)

Population
20,229,000

Product per person
$41,205

DID YOU KNOW?

Reykjavik is the capital of Iceland. It has a population of just 120,000. The city traditionally relied on fishing, but recently tourism and industry have become more important. Iceland is a good place to see the spectacular Northern Lights.

NORTHERN LIGHTS

The Sami people live in northern Norway, Sweden and Finland. Traditionally they lived by herding reindeer and sheep, and by fishing. Today, about 90% of Sami work in forestry, tourism and other industries, but they make great efforts to preserve their culture.

Germany

Germany is a democratic republic occupying a key position in central Europe.

The German people have inhabited this area for more than 2,000 years, but they did not come together to form a single country until 1870. Germany is one of the most industrialized and wealthiest countries in Europe. It is a key member of the European Union.

Happy Journey

BRANDENBURG GATE

COOL FACT!

The motor vehicle industry in Germany has been a major employer for 100 years. The luxury cars produced by Mercedes-Benz are considered to be among the best in the world. Other German car companies include BMW, Audi and Volkswagen.

-WESTFALEN GERMANY
-07-11
498485

Mercedes-Benz

Berlin is the capital of Germany. In 1788 the old city walls were demolished and replaced with parks and wide streets. The main gate into the city, the Brandenburg Gate, was rebuilt to look like a classical temple, and is now one of the most famous landmarks in the city.

The Euro currency came into being in 2002. It was adopted by 17 of the 27 countries in the European Union – these gave up their old currencies. Some 332 million Europeans use the currency every day. The Euro is now the second-largest currency in the world after the US Dollar.

AMAZING!

Neuschwanstein Castle is one of thousands of castles and fortresses built across Germany. It may look like a medieval fortress, but it was actually built in 1892 as a luxurious palace for King Ludwig of Bavaria.

Data Bank

Area
137,846 square miles (357,021 sq km)

Population
81,800,000

Product per person
$39,000

This huge bucket-wheel excavator, or strip mining machine, was built by a German company to remove first rock and soil, and then coal, from a coal strip mine in Hambach. It is the largest land vehicle in the world.

NEUSCHWANSTEIN

DID YOU KNOW?

Hitler
In 1933, after a period of political upheavals, Adolf Hitler became dictator of Germany as leader of the Nazi Party. In 1939 Hitler ordered the German army to invade Poland, thus starting the Second World War, which was to cause about 70 million deaths and leave most of Europe in ruins.

VISIT EUROPE · VISIT EUROPE · VISIT EURO

Alpine Countries

Switzerland and Austria

The Alps are a mountain chain that stretches across the top of Italy in southern central Europe.

Parts of these mountains lie in various countries, but two countries lie largely within the Alps and are known as the Alpine countries: Switzerland and Austria. There is little fertile farmland in the mountains, so people here have turned to industry and finance to make their livings.

AUSTRIAN PARLIAMENT

Austria's Parliament building was built in Vienna in 1874. The structure was designed to look like a Greek temple, emphasizing that democracy had begun in Greece. Although badly damaged during the Second World War, it has now been fully restored.

FASCINATING FACTS!

- Wolfgang Amadeus Mozart (1756–1791) was born in Salzburg, Austria. He began playing the piano aged 3, and composed his first music aged 5.
- A child genius, Mozart toured Europe giving concerts. He wrote over 600 works, characterized by their passion, joy, simplicity and grace.

The Matterhorn is a dramatic, triangular mountain in southern Switzerland. The summit is 4,478 m (14,691 ft) above sea level. It is one of the most dangerous mountains to climb – about 500 people have died on it since 1865.

Data Bank

Area
48,305 square miles (125,110 sq km)

Population
15,860,000

Product per person
$43,000

Skiing and tourism are major employers in the Alps. Every year, hundreds of thousands of people visit the Alps to ski on the snow-covered slopes. In 2011, Switzerland announced it had catered for 28 million "skier days" the previous winter.

DID YOU KNOW?

High-quality watches and clocks have been made in Switzerland since the early 19th century. Among the more famous companies today are Omega, Longines, Tissot and Breguet. In addition, fun, novelty watches are made by Swatch.

Happy Journey

Swiss Emmenthal cheese

Baltic States

The Baltic States are the three countries that occupy the east coast of the Baltic Sea: Estonia, Latvia and Lithuania.

The climate here is cold in the winter and warm in the summer. Much of the area was originally covered by forest, but farmland now covers large areas. The region remained agricultural until late into the 20th century, when industrialization began.

TALLINN

Tallinn is the capital of Estonia. The oldest structure in the city is St Olaf's Church, built about 1190. The spire stands 125 m (410 ft) tall. It has been hit by lightning at least 10 times.

AMAZING!

Skype software was released in 2003 by an Estonian computer company. It allows people to speak to each other using their computers as video phones. Skype now has 664 million users.

DID YOU KNOW?

Caraway cheese
A delicacy of the Baltic States is caraway cheese – a low-fat, spreadable cheese flavored with caraway seeds. The cheese is often melted over boiled potatoes.

Data Bank

Area
198,239 square miles (513,439 sq km)

Population
11,826,000

Product per person
$32,545

The Baltic Sea is linked to the North Sea by a narrow channel, so the waters cannot move much. In winter, when temperatures fall, the trapped water freezes. Between December and April about 45% of the Baltic is frozen, and ships cannot use it.

AMAZING!

The geographic center of Europe, according to the Lithuanian government, is a field near Bernotai, Lithuania. Not everyone agrees, as it depends whether or not outlying islands, such as the Faroes, are included.

Tartu is the second-largest city in Estonia, with a population of 102,000. Every year it holds a Medieval festival to celebrate its roots as a Hanseatic trading city (the Hanseatic League was a trading alliance in northern Europe from the 13th to 17th centuries).

Southern and Eastern Europe

Southern and eastern Europe includes those countries that border the Mediterranean Sea and the Black Sea, or rivers that drain into them.

In this Atlas, Russia and Turkey, which straddle Europe and Asia, are covered in the Asia region.

FASCINATING FACTS

- Rome is the capital of Italy. It was formerly the center of the largest empire of the ancient world.
- The Roman Empire stretched from northern Britain to southern Egypt, and from the Atlantic Ocean to the Black Sea.

VISAS 11

Stats and Facts

Countries:
Portugal, Spain, Italy, San Marino, Vatican City, Malta, Cyprus, Croatia, Greece, Bulgaria, Romania, Moldova, Ukraine, Belarus, Poland, Czech Republic, Slovakia, Hungary, Slovenia, Serbia, Albania, Bosnia-Herzegovina, Montenegro, Macedonia and Kosovo.

Tallest Mountain:
Mulhacén, Spain, 3,481 m (11,421 ft).
Note: Pico de Teide, on the Spanish island of Tenerife, is higher at 3,718 m (12,198 ft), but Tenerife is geographically part of Africa.

Porto
Duero
PORTUGAL
PYRENEES
ANDORRA
Tajo (Tagus)
Madrid
Lisbon
Barcelona
Guadiana
SPAIN
MEDITERRANEAN SEA

AMAZING!

Kosovo
In 2008 Kosovo declared itself independent of Serbia, but Serbia still controls part of the country and not every country recognizes that Kosovo is independent.

The inland countries of eastern Europe have hot summers, but their winters are usually freezing.

The steppes of the Ukraine are vast open plains, once grassland but now used to grow cereal crops. Ukraine is the world's third-largest exporter of grains.

The Carpathian Mountains stretch in a curve for more than 900 miles (1,500 km). They are an important refuge for wildlife, such as brown bears, wolves and lynx.

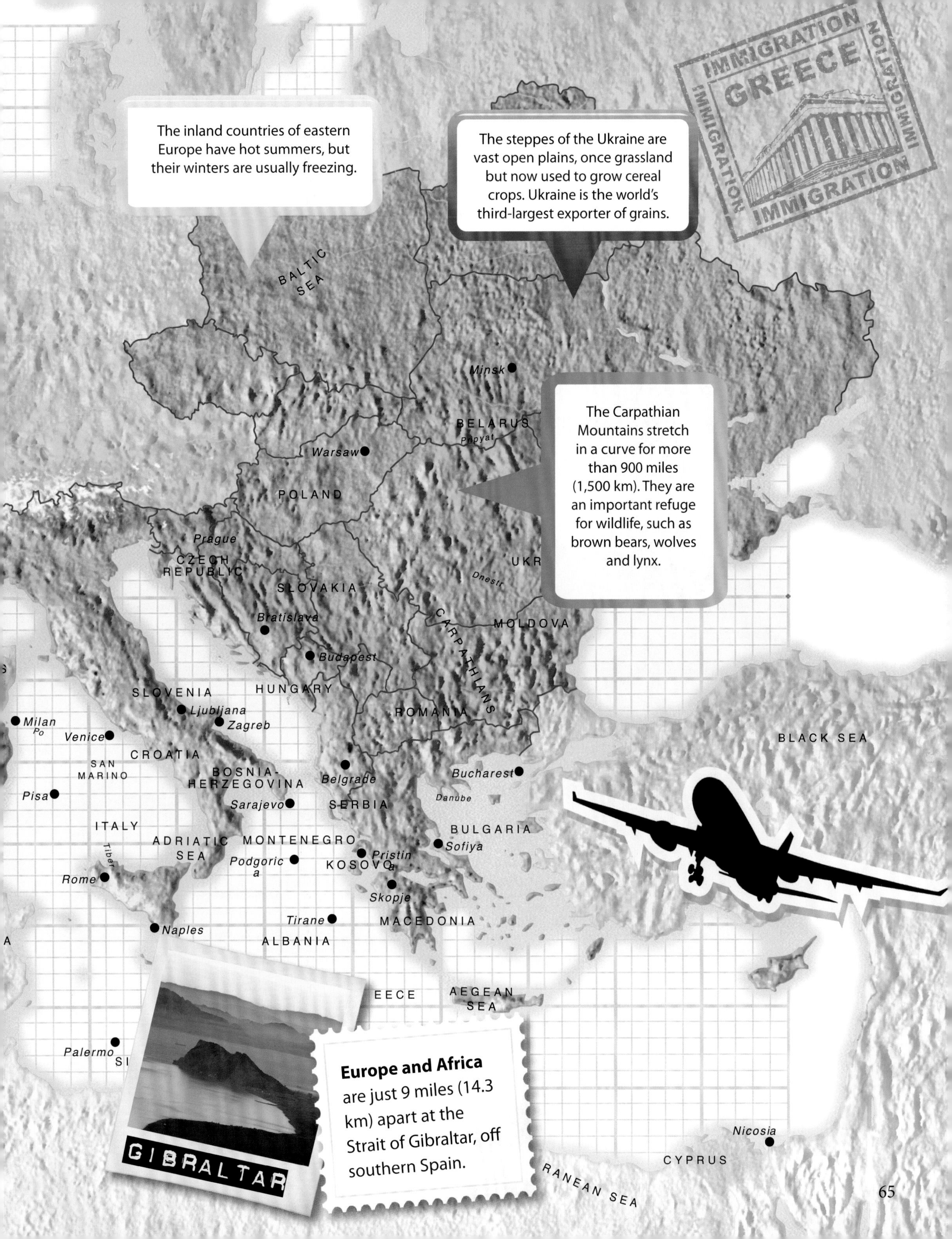

GIBRALTAR

Europe and Africa are just 9 miles (14.3 km) apart at the Strait of Gibraltar, off southern Spain.

Habitats and Wildlife

Around the Mediterranean, semi-tropical trees and flowers flourish in the mild, sunny climate. In eastern Europe, forests and grasslands are the natural vegetation.

Wildlife includes lynx, brown bears and many species of birds and insects, while lizards and tortoises bask in the sun.

Wild boar are found across the entire region, wherever there is woodland that humans do not often visit. Although they are aggressive when threatened, wild boar prefer to hide or flee from danger. All modern farm pigs are descended from wild boar.

The European brown bear is smaller than its Asian and North American relatives. It may live to be over 40 years of age. In central Italy a separate sub-species survives, with just 40 individuals left in the wild.

AMAZING!

Ibex

The ibex is a wild goat found in the mountains of southern Europe, and also in north Africa and parts of Asia. It is an agile climber, scrambling over steep rocks with ease. Ibexes have long, curving horns. They live in small herds, each led by a male.

White pelicans are fairly common on lakes, rivers and swamps across southern and southeastern Europe. They feed in small groups, surrounding a shoal of fish and then dipping their beaks into the water to trap the fish.

The black pine is common across southern Europe. This tall tree grows to about 50 m (164 ft), making it an ideal construction timber, but since the 1990s it has been planted less due to a fungal disease killing many trees.

The lynx is the biggest cat native to Europe. It hunts roe deer, rabbits, voles and any other animal that it is strong enough to kill. In southern Europe the lynx is almost extinct, but it remains numerous in the east.

Peoples

The peoples of southern and eastern Europe are diverse and come from a range of cultures.

During the Middle Ages, waves of invaders and immigrants moved from Asia or Africa into the region. Today the area is home to a number of nationalities, each with its own distinctive culture.

TRADITIONAL ROMANIAN WEDDING

In Romania, almost 90% of the inhabitants are Romanians. They have lived in this region for at least 2,000 years. The other 10% includes Hungarians, Germans and Poles.

DID YOU KNOW?

The Magyars, or Hungarians, moved into Hungary about 1,100 years ago. They were pagans who raided surrounding lands on horseback, and herded cattle. By about 1050 they had become Christian and adopted a farming lifestyle. Many Magyar retain their horse-riding skills for herding cattle.

FASCINATING FACTS

- The Roma, or Romani, sometimes called Gypsies, are a group of traveling people who left northwestern India about 1,500 years ago.
- There are now about 5 million Romani scattered across Europe, Brazil and the USA, with most living in southeastern Europe.

Flamenco is a special form of dance and music in Spain. It features guitar music, hand clapping and foot stomping, as well as abrupt, rhythmic movements. Flamenco grew out of a fusion of music of the Spanish and Romani peoples.

Most people in Sicily today speak Italian, but a small number speak Albanian and there is a strong Greek cultural heritage. The island lies in the middle of the Mediterranean Sea, at the foot of Italy.

AMAZING!

Most Greek people in southeastern Europe belong to the Greek Orthodox Church. It was an accepted institution under the Ottoman Empire (Turkish rule) and has helped to define their nationality.

GREEK ORTHODOX CHURCH

Iberia

The Iberian peninsula lies to the south of the Pyrenees. It is occupied by Spain and Portugal.

The climate is generally warm and fairly dry, with hot summers and cool winters. The area has an advanced industrial economy and its people are prosperous. Tourism is important in both countries. In Portugal, people flock to the Algarve – an area in the south famous for its beaches, oranges, figs and almonds. Spain's Costa del Sol also has popular resorts and beaches, as well as 300 days of sunshine a year. In 2012, 9.1 million people vacationed there.

Madrid, Spain's capital, is the largest city in Iberia. During the 20th century it developed as a major industrial center, but in the 21st century services such as banking, insurance and tourism became more important.

MADRID

The Alhambra is a fortified palace in the Spanish city of Granada, famous for its intricate decorations. It was built in the 14th century, at a time when much of southern Iberia was ruled by the Muslim Moors from North Africa.

The **Alqueva dam** in southern Portugal was completed in 2012 and is the largest dam in Europe. It holds back a 96 square mile (250 sq km) lake, used for water sports and to supply water to industry, farms and towns.

Data Bank

Area
224,507 square miles (581,471 sq km)

Population
55 million

Highest Point
Mulhacén, Spain, 3,478.6 m (11,413 ft)

Longest River
Tagus, 645 miles (1,038 km)

Don Quixote statue, Madrid

FASCINATING FACTS

- Grapes grown in the Douro River valley in northern Portugal are used to make port wine.
- Port is named for the city of Oporto, where the wine is bottled.
- About 14 million bottles of port are produced each year.

Italy

The boot-shaped peninsular that extends south from the Alps is occupied by the Republic of Italy, together with the small states of San Marino and Vatican City.

Until AD 476, Italy was the center of the vast Roman Empire, but waves of barbarian invaders divided the area up into a number of small countries. Italy was united again in 1871. It now has a diverse economy and is famous for its artistic heritage and cuisine.

The Vatican is a tiny state that covers just 0.17 square miles (0.44 sq km) in central Rome. It is ruled by the pope and houses the central administration of the Roman Catholic Church.

AMAZING!

The Renaissance was the artistic revolution that took place during the 15th and 16th centuries, starting in Italy and spreading to the rest of Europe. It was a "rebirth" of ancient styles from the Roman Empire, but included dramatic innovations. Leonardo da Vinci is the most famous Renaissance artist.

The Colosseum in Rome was built to hold more than 50,000 people, and was the venue for gladiator combats, animal hunts and the execution of criminals. As well as ancient ruins, the Roman Empire left behind a heritage of law codes, language and culture.

FIAT, TURIN

The bell tower of the cathedral in Pisa was completed in 1372. Because it was built on soft ground, it began to lean. Massive engineering works were carried out (1990–2008) to stop the Leaning Tower of Pisa falling over.

The Fiat car company is based in Turin. Fiat make cars, trucks and machinery. The company employs 214,000 people in more than 100 countries. In 2012 it made a profit of 1.3 billion Euros.

Data Bank

Area
116,347 square miles (301,338 sq km)

Population
59,531,000

Longest river
Po, 405 miles (652 km)

Happy Journey

Western Balkans

The Western Balkans include the countries of Macedonia, Albania, Kosovo, Montenegro, Serbia, Bosnia-Herzegovina and Slovenia.

Until the 1990s these countries, apart from Albania, formed part of Yugoslavia. That country then broke up in a series of wars and revolutions that cost thousands of lives. The area is generally mountainous with a warm climate.

Belgrade, the capital of Serbia since 1842, has a population of 1.2 million, making it the biggest city in the region. Its economy is based on food processing and computer industries.

Lake Skadar lies on the border between Montenegro and Albania. It grows and shrinks considerably depending on the amount of rain that has fallen on the surrounding hills. Skadar is home to 270 bird species.

The Dinaric Alps are an offshoot of the Alps, running along the east coast of the Adriatic Sea. The mountains are very rugged and steep, making travel inland from the coast difficult. The area is thinly populated, apart from a few mining towns.

DINARIC ALPS

AMAZING!

Olive trees

Olive trees grow throughout the western Balkans. Raw olives are usually soaked in salted water for weeks before being eaten. Today, most olives grown in the region are pressed to extract olive oil – one tree can produce 2.3 kg (5 lb) of oil a year.

Lake Bled in Slovenia is famous for watersports. It hosted the World Rowing Championships in 1966, 1979, 1989 and 2011. The lake contains an island, on which stands the famous church of St Mary. It is considered good luck for a groom to carry his bride up the 99 steps to the church!

Tivat airport in Montenegro is one of the busiest airports in the region. It was built in 1974 and expanded in 2007, and now handles 5,000 flights and 750,000 passengers a year.

Romania, Bulgaria, Greece, Cyprus

Eastern Balkans

The countries of the Eastern Balkans are part of the European Union. The landscape is mountainous, but less rugged than the western Balkans, and has some fertile plains.

AMAZING!

The Trakia Highway opened in Bulgaria in 2013. This 223 mile (360 km) long highway runs from the capital, Sofia, to the Black Sea port of Burgas, by way of the city of Plovdiv. It is expected to boost industry and trade, leading to new jobs and economic improvements.

The Danube River flows from southwestern Germany across the northern and central Balkans to enter the Black Sea. It drains water from 19 countries, and has for centuries been an important trade route.

The island of Cyprus is divided in two by a "buffer zone" patrolled by United Nations soldiers. This zone separates the Greek Cypriot-controlled south from the Turkish Cypriot-controlled north.

FASCINATING FACTS

- The Romanian company Softwin, in Bucharest, became successful after developing the BitDefender anti-virus software in 1996.
- The Palace of the Parliament in Bucharest is the biggest office building in Europe and the second-biggest in the world after the US Pentagon.

UN BUFFER ZONE, CYPRUS

Limassol on Cyprus is one of the busiest ports in the Mediterranean. The Old Harbour is used by fishing boats, the New Harbour by large commercial ships and the Marina by yachts.

The Parthenon is one of the greatest treasures of Ancient Greece and one of the world's greatest cultural monuments. This great temple to the goddess Athene was built on the Acropolis in Athens in 438 BC.

Hungary, Czech Rep, Slovakia, Poland

Central Europe

The countries of Central Europe are generally said to include Hungary, Poland, the Czech Republic and Slovakia. (Sometimes Germany, Austria and Switzerland are also included.)

The Catholic Church has traditionally played an important part in the countries of Central Europe. They also share an agricultural past.

DID YOU KNOW?

Prague, capital of the Czech Republic, was once capital of the Holy Roman Empire, which lasted from AD 800 to 1806. One of its most notable features is the historic Charles Bridge, which crosses the Vltava River.

Mount Snezka straddles the border between Poland and the Czech Republic. It stands 1,602 m (5,256 ft) tall, and is topped by a restaurant and post office – postcards sent from here can be stamped "Snezka," for collectors!

The crown made for the coronation of Prince Stephen of Hungary in the year 1000 was used by all subsequent kings of Hungary, and is now in the national museum in Budapest. The cross on top was bent in the 17th century, when the crown was accidentally dropped.

The Czech company Ceske Energeticke Zavody (CEZ) is a major electricity generating business that operates across Albania, Bulgaria, Germany, Hungary, Poland, Romania, Slovakia and Turkey.

The European bison, or wisent, is a wild form of cattle. This hefty beast was hunted to extinction in the wild in Central Europe, but has been successfully reintroduced to the forests from captive stock.

AMAZING!

The Rubik's cube puzzle was invented in 1974 by Hungarian Erno Rubik.

Belarus, Ukraine, Moldova

Eastern Europe

Eastern Europe includes the countries of Belarus, Ukraine and Moldova.

For centuries these countries were ruled by Russia, and then in the 20th century by the Soviet Union. They became independent of Russia in 1991. The countries share economic problems caused by years of Communist rule, but are now making efforts to adopt more modern economic activities.

Capriana in Moldova is one of the oldest Christian sites in Eastern Europe. The monastery was founded sometime before 1429, but the current building dates from 1491.

The Antonov Aeronautical Company made transport aircraft for the Soviet government. Since independence, aircraft design and manufacturing have been upgraded to meet international standards, and Antonov aircraft are now valuable exports for Ukraine.

SCAN ME
Instructions on page 5

The Victoria Falls on the Zambezi River lie on the border between Zimbabwe and Zambia. At 108 m (355 ft) tall and 1,708 m (5,604 ft) wide, these are the largest waterfalls in the world. The flow of water varies greatly from the rainy season to the dry season.

Luanda in Angola has a population of about 5.2 million – nearly one in three of all Angolans live in the city. The large port and natural harbor are used to export products from inland, such as coffee, cotton and tobacco. Many of these goods are processed in the city before export, providing extra jobs.

Southern Africa

Southern Africa is generally drier and cooler than the Congo Basin to the north. The countries of the region lie around the Tropic of Capricorn. They include Namibia, Botswana, Zimbabwe, South Africa, Lesotho and Swaziland.

Until 1994, South Africa was governed by a system that allowed only white people to vote in elections and enjoy full economic freedoms. In 1994, all citizens gained the vote. The first president under the new system was Nelson Mandela, who led the struggle for full democracy.

DRAKENSBERG

The highest range of mountains in southern Africa is the Drakensberg in South Africa. It rises to 3,482 m (11,424 ft) at Mount Thabana Ntlenyana. The mountains are a popular holiday destination because of the beautiful scenery and excellent walking trails.

AMAZING!

Boerewors

A traditional food of South Africa is the Boerewors. This sausage is made of coarsely minced beef mixed with coriander, pepper, nutmeg, cloves and vinegar. It is traditionally grilled and served with bread or a porridge made from cornmeal.

AMAZING!

Vast deposits of gold ore were found, in 1884, in what is now South Africa. The country now accounts for about 14% of world gold production and has over 50% of known deposits of gold ore. The Tau Tona gold mine is over 2.4 miles (3.9 km) deep, making it the deepest mine in the world.

Grasslands known as veldt cover much of southern Africa. Flat plains and gentle hills are typical, but in places there are deep gorges and rocky hills. Gazelle, lions, elephants and other large animals graze on the veldt. Large areas are also used to graze cattle.

Happy Journey

The Namib Desert stretches for nearly 1,250 miles (2,000 km) from north to south along the southwest coast of Africa. The desert is home to the welwitschia plant, which grows nowhere else, and has not changed since the time of the dinosaurs.

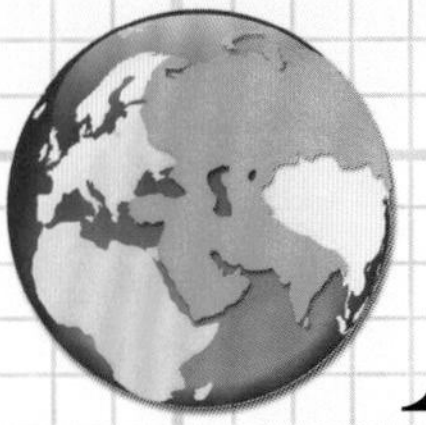

West, Central and South Asia

This region contains some of the most densely populated lands on Earth, as well as some of the most rugged, wild and least populated.

Across part of the region, two of the Earth's tectonic plates are colliding, and this has created the mighty Himalaya mountain range between India and China. The range is 1,500 miles (2,400 km) long and up to 250 miles (400 km) wide. The mountains form a barrier to animals and people moving between India and the rest of Asia.

Stats and Facts

Countries:
India, Nepal, Bhutan, Sri Lanka, Afghanistan, Pakistan, Bangladesh, Maldives, Russia, Georgia, Armenia, Azerbaijan, Turkmenistan, Kazakhstan, Kyrgyzstan, Tajikistan, Uzbekistan, Iran, Iraq, Kuwait, Bahrain, Qatar, United Arab Emirates, Oman, Yemen, Saudi Arabia, Israel, Syria, Lebanon, Jordan, Turkey.

Highest point
Mount Everest 8,848 m (29,029 ft)

Lowest point
Dead Sea -427 m (-1,400 ft) (below sea level)

The Himalayas form the highest mountain range in the world. They began to form about 15 million years ago and are still rising.

The Ural Mountains form the boundary between Europe and the rest and Asia (Russia straddles both continents). They are a rich source of minerals, such as coal, copper ore and gemstones.
The Caspian Sea is the largest body of water not connected to the open ocean in the world. Some scientists consider it to be a sea, others think it is a salt lake.
Across western Asia, closely related animals have adapted to very different environments. Siberian tigers live in snowy forests, while Indian tigers hunt in hot swamps and jungles.
Lake Baikal in Siberia is the deepest lake in the world, reaching 1,642 m (5,387 ft) deep. It contains about 20% of the world's unfrozen fresh water.
LAKE BAIKAL
Bering Sea
Kara Sea
Laptev Sea
St Petersburg
Moscow
Kazan
Nordvik
CENTRAL SIBERIAN PLATEAU
Siberian Lowland
RUSSIA
Lensk
Novosibirsk
Irkutsk
Lake Baykal
SAYAN MTS.
Kabul
HINDU KUSH
Vladivostok
Aral Sea
KYRGYZSTAN
TAJIKISTAN
Tashkent
Bishkek
Dushanbe
Islamabad
(disputed area)
Lahore
HIMALAYAS
Delhi
NEPAL
Kathmandu
Mt. Everest
BHUTAN
Thimphu
INDIA
BANGLADESH
Kolkata (Calcutta)
Dhaka
Hyderabad
Bay of Bengal
Chennai (Madras)
SRI LANKA
Colombo
INDIAN OCEAN
RÉPUBLIQUE DE MADAGASCAR

Habitats and Wildlife

Stretching across the north of the region is a vast belt of taiga forest, also known as boreal forest. Here, evergreen pines, firs and other trees densely cover the land for thousands of miles.

Lampreys, blackfish, pike and other taiga fish are adapted to surviving in the deep cold of ice-covered waters. Salmon and trout retreat to the warmer seas to escape the cold winters.

Brown bears and other taiga mammals eat vast quantities of food during the summer to build up thick layers of fat for the winter. In winter the bears hibernate, and their bodies absorb the fat. Bison and reindeer grow thick coats of fur to protect them from the cold.

The trees and other plants have a summer growing season of less than four months, and in some areas as little as two months, when temperatures are above 10°C (50°F). For the rest of the year, when the average daytime temperature is -15°C (5°F), it is too cold for plants to grow. Despite the short summers and long winters, the taiga supports a wide variety of plants and animals.

Conifers, such as pine, fir and spruce, are the most numerous trees in the taiga. Areas that escape the coldest winter weather support a wider range of trees, including larch, willow, alder and poplar.

AMAZING!

Verkhoyansk, in the taiga belt, is the coldest place in the northern hemisphere. On 7 February, 1892, temperatures plunged to -67.7°C (-89.86°F).

DID YOU KNOW?

Cold for birds

Birds of the taiga usually fly in for the summer to feed on plants or insects, and then fly south to warmer regions during the winter. Of the estimated 300 species of bird to be found in the taiga in the summer, only about 30 remain for the winter.

Peoples

This region has an amazing variety of peoples, from the remote reindeer herders of icy Siberia to the teeming millions in the cities of southern India.

Across Central Asia, historic trade routes connected East, South and Western Asia with Europe, making it a crossroads for the movement of people, goods and ideas.

The Iranian peoples number about 150 million. Most Iranians are Muslims, but some are Christians or Zoroastrians. As well as the Iranians themselves, other peoples who speak a form of Iranian language are the Kurds, Laks and Baluchis.

In India, sadhu are wandering Hindu holy men who devote their lives to contemplation of the ultimate reality of infinite being, or brahman. Most sadhu have renounced all possessions. There are thought to be about 2 million sadhu in India today.

IRANIANS

AMAZING!

Turks

The Turkish peoples originally came from Central Asia near the Caspian Sea, but they gradually moved west and now live primarily in Turkey. During the 16th century the Turks ruled an empire that stretched from near Vienna to the Indian Ocean, and included most of North Africa.

TAJIK WOMAN

Siberia in northern Russia was traditionally inhabited by nomadic peoples who lived a hunter-gatherer lifestyle. These peoples are now outnumbered about 10 to 1 by Russians, who have moved to Siberia to work in mines and industry.

The Tajiks, or Farsi, are a people of south Central Asia who live mostly in Tajikistan and Uzbekistan. They number about 16 million. These peoples speak a form of Persian language and follow the Islamic religion.

The Arabs are a people who originally lived in the Arabian Peninsula. After their conversion to the Islamic faith, the Arabs swept out of Arabia to conquer neighboring countries, reaching as far as Spain and the Himalayas. In many of these countries, the local people adopted Islam and the Arab language.

Nepal, Bhutan, Sri Lanka and India

The Indian subcontinent lies south of the Himalayas. It includes the island chain of the Maldives in the Indian Ocean.

Most of the inhabitants of this area share cultural traits, though the region is firmly divided between the Hindu and Islamic religions.

Tea is grown on plantations, called tea gardens, in India, Nepal and Sri Lanka. India is the second-largest producer of tea in the world after China. About 70% of India's tea is consumed by Indians themselves.

The Harmandir Sahib, or Golden Temple, in Amritsar is the holiest temple of the Sikhs. It was built in 1574, and was covered with gold in the 1830s. The temple stands at the center of an artificial lake.

Kathmandu is the capital of Nepal, which has a population of about 26 million and is located high up in the Himalayas. In 2008 King Gyanendra was forced to give up his throne and Nepal became a republic.

AMAZING!

Cricket
Cricket was brought to India in the 1830s by Englishmen working for the East India Company. Today, it is a passion throughout India, Pakistan, Sri Lanka and Bangladesh, and is played at international level.

The Taj Mahal at Agra, India, is widely acknowledged to be one of the most beautiful buildings in the world. It was built of white marble in 1653 by the ruler Shah Jahan as a memorial to his wife Mumtaz Mahal.

Mount Everest is the tallest mountain on Earth. It stands at 8,848 m (29,029 ft) above sea level on the border between Nepal and China. The local name for the mountain is Sagarmatha, which means "Holy Mother."

TAJ MAHAL

Pakistan, Bangladesh and Afghanistan

Exceptionally rugged, steep mountains lie to the northeast and northwest of the Indian sub-continent.

In this part of the region there are few valleys with good soil for farming, and only limited mineral deposits worth mining. The lands are generally poor and sparsely populated. The main religion is Islam. There have been several wars here in recent years.

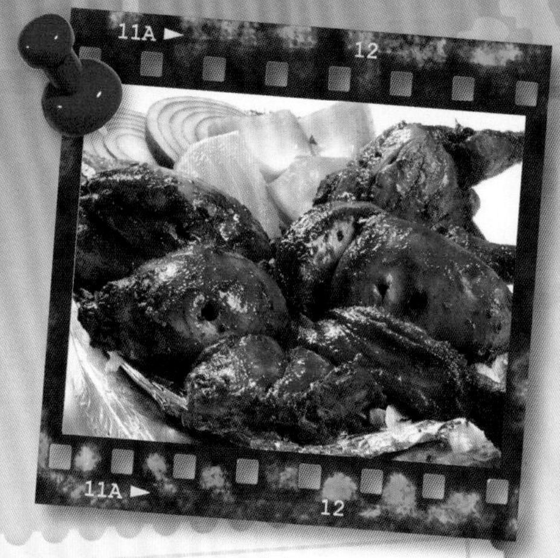

A tandoor is a clay pot or oven used across southern, central and western Asia for cooking bread or marinated meat. The charcoal or wood flavors the food.

The Friday Mosque in Herat, Afghanistan, was built during the 1440s and is famous for the colorful glazed tiles that cover much of the building. It fell into disrepair during the 20th century, when wars wracked Afghanistan, but is now being repaired.

Extensive mangrove swamps have formed at the mouths of several large rivers flowing out of Pakistan and Bangladesh. The roots and trunks of the mangrove trees stand in salty water and form a dense network that is impenetrable to people.

The railway network of the Indian subcontinent was crucial to the economic development of the region during the 19th and 20th centuries. The role of rail has declined since 1980, but it remains an important industry, moving millions of people and freight daily across a challenging landscape.

Tigers once roamed across most of Asia, but they are now restricted to a few small areas of forest. There are an estimated 1,700–1,900 Bengal tigers in India, 440 in Bangladesh, 124–229 in Nepal and 67–81 in Bhutan. Since 2010, the Bengal tiger has been classified as an endangered species.

SCAN ME

Instructions on page 5

Russia

Russia is the largest country in the world, covering 6,592,848 square miles (17,075,400 sq km) of northern Europe and Asia.

Such a vast area has a wide variety of landscapes, from Arctic tundra to fertile farmland and towering mountains. It is also home to two of the greatest cities in the world: Moscow (population 11.5 million) and St Petersburg (4.9 million).

PUTIN

AMAZING!

As Prime Minister of Russia (1999–2000), Vladimir Putin was credited with restoring political stability and economic growth. He held this office again from 2008 to 2012, then became President for a second time.

St Petersburg on the Baltic Sea is the cultural capital of Russia, as well as being an important port and military base. The city was founded in 1703 by the Russian ruler Peter the Great, and named in his honor.

Data Bank

Area
6,592,800 square miles (17,076,000 sq km)

Population
143,300,000

Highest Point
Mount Elbrus 5,642 m (18,510 ft)

Longest River
Volga, 2,294 miles (3,692 km)

The Kremlin is a fortress in the center of Moscow, the Russian capital. It was first built in 1090 and enlarged to its present size in 1495. The Kremlin houses palaces, churches and offices used by the government.

DID YOU KNOW?

Coal-fired power plants, such as this one in Moscow, account for about 29% of Russia's electricity generation. A 75% increase in coal production is anticipated by 2020. Russia is the world's largest exporter of oil and gas, transporting large amounts of both through pipelines to other countries.

AMAZING!

St Basil's Cathedral is a magnificent Christian church overlooking Red Square in Moscow. Eight brightly painted chapels surround the tall, central structure. In 1929 the Communist government confiscated the building from the Orthodox Church and converted it into a museum.

Central Asia

Central Asia stretches from Afghanistan north to Russia and from China west to the Caspian Sea.

It is occupied by the five "stans" – Kazakhstan, Kyrgyzstan, Tajikistan, Turkmenistan and Uzbekistan. From the early 19th century until 1991 these countries were under Russian rule, first as part of the Russian Empire, then as part of the Soviet Union. Today the region is poor, but the people are proud of their national identities and traditional clothes and customs are making a comeback.

Plov is a common dish made by boiling rice in meat broth, then adding pieces of meat and vegetables. It is often served with side dishes of dried fruits and nuts.

NUR-ASTANA MOSQUE

The largest mosque in Central Asia is the Nur-Astana Mosque in Astana, capital of Kazakhstan. It can hold 5,000 people. Most people in Central Asia are Muslim.

ASTANA

Data Bank

Area
1,545,566 square miles (4,003,000 sq km)

Population
64.8 million

Product per person
$2,700

Ashgabat is the capital and largest city of Turkmenistan. In 1948 the city was almost totally destroyed by an earthquake, but it was rapidly rebuilt. Most of the people in the city work for the government, though some factories process local agricultural products.

The Kazakh government has spent vast sums of money gained from the oil industry on building new streets, offices and houses in the country's capital, Astana. Many of the buildings have been completed to dramatic and innovative designs.

Happy Journey

Iran, Iraq and the smaller Gulf States

The Persian Gulf was, in the past, a fairly poor area with little agriculture and few resources.

Most people lived by fishing, pearl fishing or working the trade routes between India and Europe. The discovery of vast oil and gas fields in the last 60 years has transformed the region, providing wealth and employment in vast quantities. The smaller Gulf States are Bahrain, Kuwait, Qatar and the United Arab Emirates. Saudi Arabia and Oman are the two larger Gulf states, also known as Arabia.

Political instability has been a feature of the Gulf region for most of the past century. There have been several wars, revolutions and rebellions. All the states maintain large military forces. The United Arab Emirates, for example, has a permanent military of 65,000 men, plus another 412,000 reservists, out of a total population of 7 million people.

The Khalifa Stadium in Doha, Qatar, is the center of a sports complex that includes training grounds, swimming pools, tracks and other facilities. The 2006 Asian Games and 2011 Asian Cup were among the major sporting events held here.

FASCINATING FACTS

- Iran has long been famous for its handwoven carpets, often called Persian carpets, as Iran was formerly known as Persia.
- In 2008, Iran sold $420 million worth of carpets abroad. The carpet industry employs about 1.2 million people.

QUALITY AVIATION

AMAZING!

The Arabian oryx is an antelope with impressive horns up to 1 m (3 ft) long. Due to hunting by humans, it became extinct in the wild in 1972, but in 1980 some zoo oryx were successfully released into the wild, and the animal is no longer threatened with extinction.

ARABIAN ORYX

Oil refining and export plants are major employers in the region and are of global importance. Most of Iraq's oil exports leave from the Al Basrah Oil Terminal – a trans-shipment facility from the pipelines to the tankers. The oil is then sold and exported throughout the world.

In 2003, Iraq was invaded by an Allied force from the USA, Britain, Australia and Poland, their aim being to remove from power the Iraqi dictator Saddam Hussein and locate any Iraqi weapons of mass destruction. Iraq was quickly defeated, but there followed a long period of rebellions, revolts and terrorism. The USA kept troops in Iraq until 2011.

Saudi Arabia, Oman, Yemen

Arabia

Arabia is a vast area of desert and arid lands that form a peninsula between Africa and the mainland of Asia.

The region has few rivers or lakes, but there are numerous valleys with temporary streams and underground sources of water, making farming possible. Livestock are herded across areas where grasses or scrub will grow. In the 1930s, oil was discovered in Arabia, bringing huge wealth to the region.

Riyadh is the capital of Saudi Arabia, the largest country in Arabia. The Saud Dynasty, a family of nobles from Riyadh, founded the new kingdom of Saudi Arabia in 1932. Saudi Arabia is immensely wealthy due to it having the world's second-largest oil reserves, after Venezuela.

Many women in Arabia wear a niqab (a cloth to cover the face) and a hijab (a cloth over the hair) when out in public. Together these leave only the eyes visible to any men who are not members of the family. Opinion is divided as to whether wearing the niqab is a religious duty or not.

SULTAN OF OMAN

NIQAB

Oman is ruled by a sultan of the Al Said dynasty, which dates back to 1744. Although Oman is a major oil and gas producer, the country is seeking to establish other industries to take over when the oil runs out.

AMAZING!

Date palms have been farmed in Arabia for at least 6,000 years. The trees thrive in hot climates and need less water than other trees. Dates contain a high quantity of vitamins, and can be easily dried for storage. Saudi Arabia produces about 1.2 million tonnes (1.3 million tons) of dates annually.

AMAZING!

The Mosque of the Prophet in Medina, Saudi Arabia, is the second-holiest site for Muslims after Mecca. It was founded in 622 by the Prophet Muhammad himself, who is buried there. In the 1990s it was massively expanded to house the huge number of annual pilgrims.

Ships called dhows were traditionally used by Arabians to transport goods between India and Europe. The larger dhows had a crew of about 30 people, and carried heavy items such as fruit, fresh water and other goods.

The Middle East

The countries of Israel, Syria, Lebanon, Turkey and the proposed Palestinian State occupy an area of southwest Asia commonly known in the West as the Middle East.

The landscape is a mix of mountains, plains, deserts and fertile farmland. It is bounded by the Mediterranean Sea to the west, the Black Sea to the north, the Arabian desert to the south and the valleys of the Tigris and Euphrates to the east.

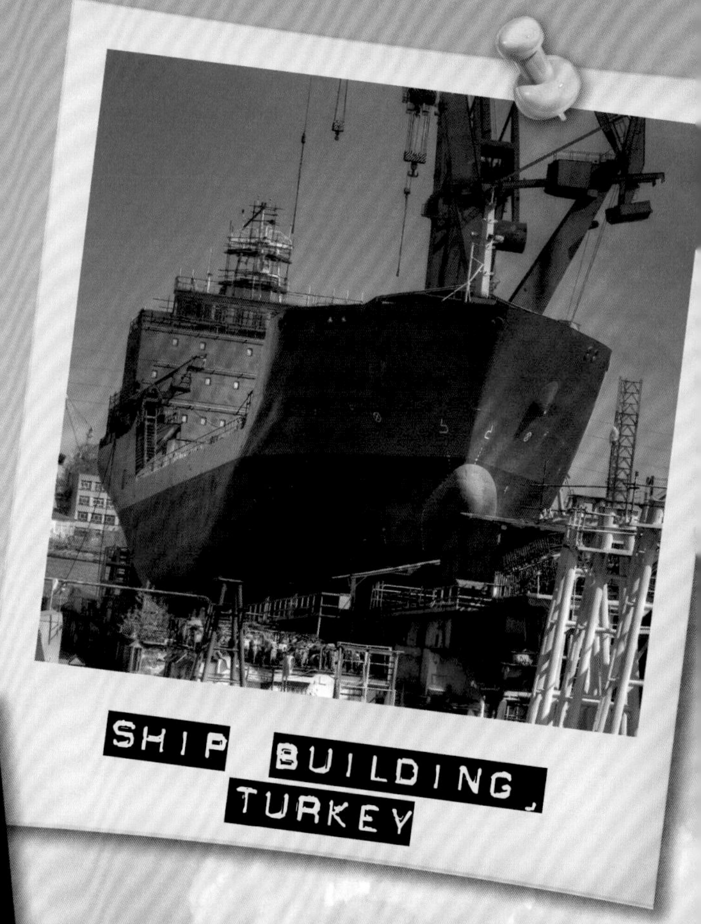

SHIP BUILDING, TURKEY

The Hagia Sophia in Istanbul, capital of Turkey, was built as a Christian church in 537. It became a mosque in 1453 and then a museum in 1935. Istanbul has a population of 13.8 million. Before 1453, the city, then called Constantinople, was capital of the Byzantine Empire for over 1,000 years.

Turkey is a major industrialized country. It produced more than 1 million road vehicles in 2012, while the shipbuilding industry built $1.2 billion worth of craft for export. The boom in industry has encouraged many people from small, rural villages to move into the growing towns.

AMAZING!

Oil was discovered in Syria in 1918, but did not become a major industry until the 1970s due to technical drilling problems. About 40% of Syria's product comes from oil or gas. Tourism and other businesses have suffered from the civil war that began in 2012.

The Western Wall in Jerusalem, also know as the Wailing Wall, is a holy place for Jews. It is what remains of the Temple built by King Solomon in about 950 BC and restored by Herod the Great in 19 BC. Jews visit the wall to pray and mourn the destruction of the Temple.

AMAZING!

Ruins of Troy

The ancient city of Troy, made famous by the poet Homer, stood at a site now called Hisarlik. It grew wealthy by controlling trade through the Dardenelles, which connect the Black Sea to the Mediterranean. Founded about 5,000 years ago, it was abandoned about 3,000 years later.

The Dome of the Rock in Jerusalem is an Islamic shrine built in about 691. It covers the rock from which Muslims believe the prophet Muhammad left Earth to visit Heaven with the angel Gabriel. The dome of the shrine is covered with 80 kg (176 lb) of gold.

WAILING WALL

East and Southeast Asia

East and Southeast Asia includes China, the world's third-largest country by area and the largest by population. This region is one of the most densely populated on the planet, with huge, crowded cities, especially in Japan and parts of Indonesia.

The Silk Road was a trade route that connected China to Europe from about 200 BC to AD 1700. Few people traveled the entire length of the road. Instead, goods were passed from one merchant to the next along the route.

VISAS 11

Stats and Facts

Countries:
China, North Korea, South Korea, Mongolia, Japan, Myanmar (Burma), Thailand, Cambodia, Laos, Vietnam, Malaysia, Singapore, Indonesia, Brunei, Philippines, East Timor.

Largest City:
Tokyo 32.5 million

Tallest Mountain:
Aksai Chin 1 (The Kunlun Goddess), 7,167 m (23,514 ft). For Mount Everest, shared by Nepal and China, see West and South Asia.

Happy Journey

AMAZING!

Krakatoa
In 1883 the volcano of Krakatoa in Indonesia erupted with a blast so loud it was heard 3,000 miles (4,800 km) away. The eruption destroyed two thirds of the island, created a huge tsunami and killed about 37,000 people.

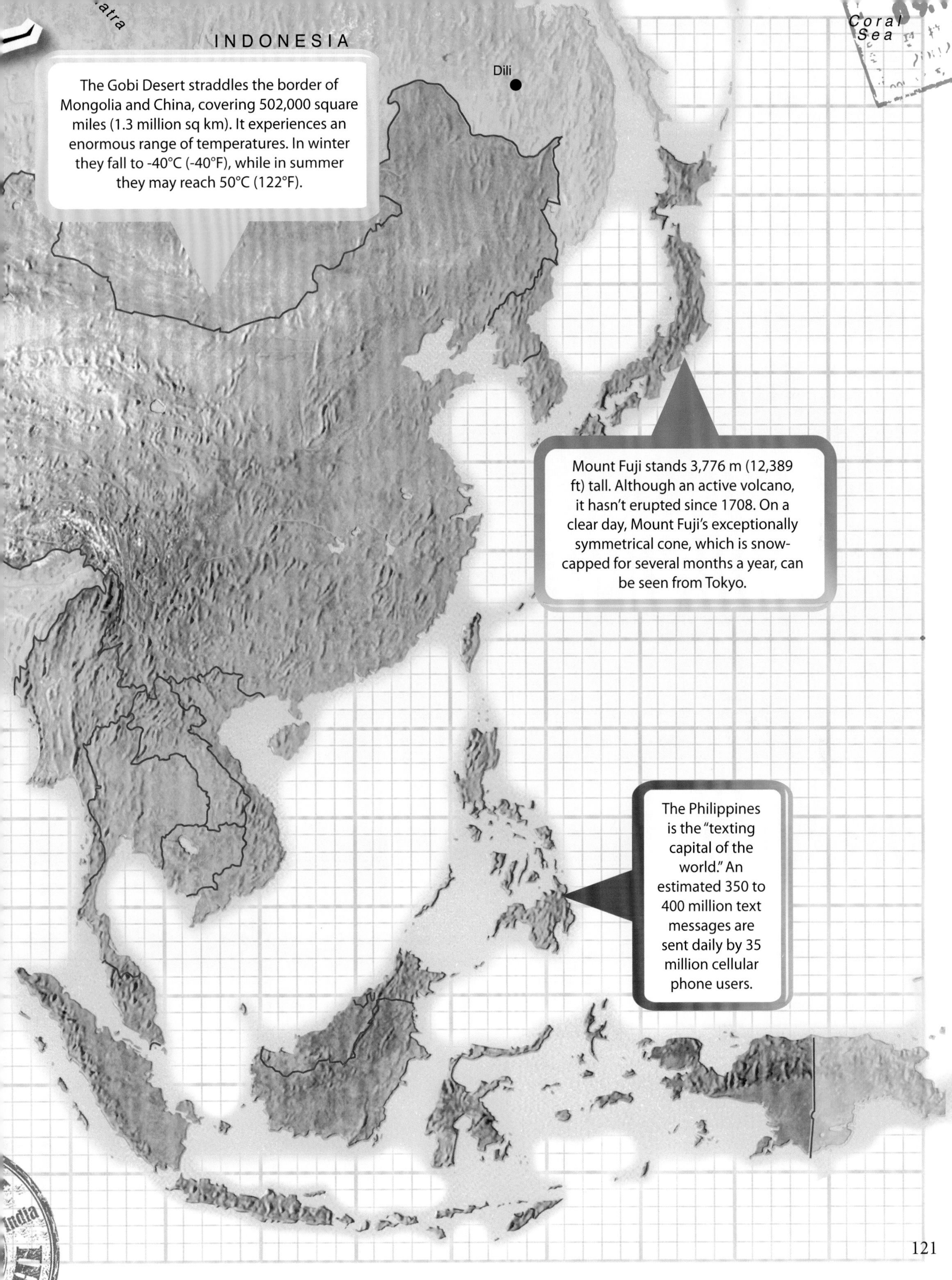

INDONESIA

Dili

Coral Sea

The Gobi Desert straddles the border of Mongolia and China, covering 502,000 square miles (1.3 million sq km). It experiences an enormous range of temperatures. In winter they fall to -40°C (-40°F), while in summer they may reach 50°C (122°F).

Mount Fuji stands 3,776 m (12,389 ft) tall. Although an active volcano, it hasn't erupted since 1708. On a clear day, Mount Fuji's exceptionally symmetrical cone, which is snow-capped for several months a year, can be seen from Tokyo.

The Philippines is the "texting capital of the world." An estimated 350 to 400 million text messages are sent daily by 35 million cellular phone users.

Habitats and Wildlife

East and Southeast Asia share the world's greatest mountain range – the mighty Himalayas. This range is home to snow leopards, Himalayan wolves and tahrs, and Tibetan bears.

To the north of the Himalayas is the world's highest and largest plateau, the Tibetan Plateau. With an average elevation exceeding 4,500 m (14,800 ft), it is sometimes called "the Roof of the World." From this plateau flows the Yangtze River, or Chang Jiang – the longest river in Asia.

The Himalayas are rising by about 5 mm (0.19 in.) each year. Like all mountains, they are also being eroded. Rainwater, wind and glaciers gradually remove tiny pieces of rock and shift them downhill. Other mountains on Earth were once taller than the Himalayas, but have been eroded to be smaller.

FASCINATING FACTS

- The Himalayan tahr is a relative of the wild goat, and is specially adapted to life in the rugged mountains.
- The snow leopard has the thickest coat of any cat. When resting, it wraps its long tail around itself like a blanet.

Volcanic eruptions are frequent along the eastern edge of Asia, which is part of the Pacific Ring of Fire. A volcano forms where molten rock, ash or gases from deep beneath the Earth's crust find their way to the surface.

Mount Fuji is just one of 118 volcanoes in Japan. It is Japan's highest volcano, and is considered one of three holy mountains. The level of seismic activity under the volcano was slightly higher than usual in 2000 and 2001.

The Pamirs are fold mountains in western China, Tajikistan and Afghanistan. The mountain chain runs in a north-south direction from the western end of the Himalayas to the Tien Shan. The highest peak is Ismail Samani, at 7,495 m (24,589 ft).

Peoples

The peoples of East and Southeast Asia belong to a rich mix of cultures. The mountains and seas of the region divide people from each other, giving rise to distinct differences of religion, dress, art and culture.

The Han are the largest group of humans on Earth, accounting for about 20% of all people living today. Most Han live in China, where they make up 92% of the population. Large numbers of Han also live in Singapore, Malaysia and Taiwan.

The 50 million Thai people form the bulk of the population in Thailand, with only a few living outside the country. Most Thai follow the Buddhist religion.

The Manchu live in northeast China. From 1644 to 1912, Manchu rulers were also the Emperors of China. The Manchu language is a form of the Tungusic language of northern Siberia, though most Manchu now speak Chinese.

AMAZING!

The Ainu people live in northern Japan and nearby islands. There are about 150,000 Ainu today. They make efforts to maintain their culture of animal worship, distinctive clothing and the Ainu language.

About 12 million Mongols live in Mongolia, China, Russia and Korea. In Medieval times the Mongols were united and ruled a great empire. Mongol culture is based on a traditional lifestyle of herding cattle, horses and sheep across the vast grasslands of Central Asia.

FASCINATING FACTS

- About 7 million Tatars live in China, Russia and Central Asia.
- The Tatars were traditionally nomadic herders living on the plains of Asia, but most settled to farming about 300 years ago.
- The Tatar language is related to Turkish.

Mongolia

Mongolia lies between China and Russia in eastern Asia.

The majority of Mongol people live outside Mongolia in neighboring countries, mostly China. Mongolia is a relatively poor country, where many people continue to follow their traditional lifestyle.

Yurts were lived in by the Mongols for at least 1,000 years. The wooden frame and felt or canvas covering can be put up or taken down in under two hours. Traditionally they were transported by camels or horses.

WRESTLING

Ulan Bator, the Mongolian capital, was founded in 1639 as a Buddhist monastery. It was not until 1913 that other people began settling here. The city now has a population of 1.7 million and is an important industrial and cultural center.

Mongolian wrestling dates back about 2,000 years. It was traditionally a way for warriors to keep fit. The aim is to get the opponent to touch the ground with any part of his body except the feet. Punching and kicking are not allowed.

SCAN ME

Instructions on page 5

Mongolia's traditional lifestyle involves herding camels, cattle, horses and sheep over the vast, grassy plains. About one-third of the population still lives this way. Livestock, milk, meat and cheese are sold at markets on the plains.

YURT

When the rains fall, grass grows along the fringes of the Gobi Desert and livestock can graze there. Since 1990 the number of livestock on the Chinese side has increased, causing soil erosion and the spread of the desert.

Data Bank

Area
603,909 square miles (1,564,115 sq km)

Population
3,179,997

Product per person
$4,743

Highest point
Tavan Bogd 4,374 m (14,350 ft)

Happy Journey

CHINA

North Korea and South Korea

The Korean Peninsula is inhabited almost exclusively by the Korean people.

Since 1945 it has been divided into Communist North Korea and capitalist South Korea. The two countries have officially been at war since 1954, though little fighting has taken place for the past 40 years.

MILITARY SOLDIER

The Hyundai engineering company was founded in South Korea in 1947. It now concentrates on manufacturing motor vehicles, producing about 1.7 million each year and employing 75,000 people. In 2012 the Hyundai Elantra was voted North American Car of the Year.

HYUNDAI

The Korean tea ceremony is a formal method of making and drinking tea with friends and family members. The ceremony is a way for hosts to show respect to their guests.

North Korea has armed forces totalling 1.21 million personnel, the fourth largest in the world. It also has a stock of nuclear weapons and a range of missiles that could reach China, Japan and nearby countries. This military parade is being held in the capital, Pyongyang. Large parts of the city are closed to foreigners.

GYEONGBOKGUNG PALACE

The great Gyeongbokgung Palace in Seoul, South Korea, was the main residence of the Joseon Dynasty that ruled Korea from the 14th century to 1897. The palace is now a tourist attraction and is undergoing major renovations.

AMAZING!

Jinju dance

The Jinju or Geommu Dance is a traditional sword dance of Korea. The dance originated among warriors about 1,400 years ago. It is performed by 8 dancers moving in a circle and is carried out by men or women.

DID YOU KNOW?

Seoul, the capital of South Korea, is described as a mega-city because it has a population of more than 10 million people. Nearly half of South Korea's entire population lives in the Seoul National Capital Area.

Japan

Japan is an island chain off the coast of northeast China. There are more than 6,000 islands in all, but only four large ones are heavily populated.

Until the 19th century the economy was based on traditional agriculture, but today Japan is one of the most industrialized countries in the world.

Warrior nobles known as Samurai ruled Japan from about 1150 to 1868. The Samurai trained exhaustively with swords, bows and pikes, becoming highly skilled with these weapons. Although the Samurai were overthrown, aspects of their culture remain strong in modern Japan.

Most Japanese wildlife is shared with adjacent areas of mainland Asia, but the Japanese macaque is found nowhere else. This monkey lives farther north than any other wild primate. In the bitter winters, it likes to keep warm by bathing in natural hot springs.

Tokyo city

The Hanammi Festival is held in Japan each spring, when the cherry blossom flowers. People gather beneath the cherry trees to enjoy the beautiful blossom and to eat meals in the open air.

SHINTO PRIEST

DID YOU KNOW?

Shinto is the traditional religion of Japan. It is not a formally organized religion, but rather a collection of local cults, rituals and practices that are loosely linked by their veneration of ancestors and nature spirits.

Data Bank

Area
145,925 square miles (377,944 sq km)

Population
127,800,000

Product per person
$36,266

Highest Point
Mount Fuji 3,776 m (12,388 ft)

AMAZING!

Sony Corporation
Sony started an electronics shop in a bomb-damaged department store building in Tokyo, in 1946. Now Sony employs 180,500 people and is a leading audio-visual, electronics and information technology company. It is also the second-largest music company in the world.

Western China

China has the largest population of any country on Earth, and is the second largest by area.

The landscapes of this vast country are highly varied, with mountains, plains, deserts, forests and grasslands all being found in abundance. The Chinese culture dates back over 3,000 years, and continues to flourish. The government is Communist.

In Tibet, good quality farmland is rare, but crops of rye, barley and potatoes are grown. The mountain slopes are grazed by yak, cattle, dzo, sheep, goats and camels. The yak is a form of long-haired cattle unique to Tibet, while the dzo is a cross between a yak and a cow.

The Potala Palace in Lhasa, Tibet, was once the residence of the Dalai Lama – the spiritual leader of Tibet. The palace was begun in 1645 and contains more than 1,000 rooms and 10,000 shrines. The Dalai Lama now lives in India and the Potala is a museum.

Qinghai Province covers 278,400 square miles (721,000 sq km) of western China. A high percentage of non-Chinese people live here, and Islam is an important religion. The 14th-century Donnguan Mosque is famous for its green and white tiled decoration and soaring minarets.

LOQUAT HARVEST

Small orchards growing apples, pears, plums, peaches and other fruit are abundant in the inland western provinces of China. As a whole, China produces about 56 million tonnes (62 million tons) of fruit each year.

Happy Journey

Northern China

Northern China, centred around the lowland plain of the Huang Ho River, is the political and cultural heart of China.

There is no fixed boundary to the region, but it is usually said to include Inner Mongolia, the cities of Beijing and Tianjin, and the provinces of Shanxi, Hebei, Liaoning, Jilin and Heilongjiang. The people who live here are mostly Han Chinese, speaking Mandarin.

Beijing has been the capital of China for most of the past 700 years. Today it has a population of more than 20 million people, and rising. Between 2002 and 2012 the population increased by 45%. One out of every three Beijing residents is a migrant from outside the city.

YELLOW RIVER

The Huang Ho, or Yellow River, is named for the vast quantities of yellow mud that it carries. The river irrigates the North China Plain, allowing millions of hectares of land to be farmed. Floods are frequent. The worst on record was in 1931, when over 3 million people were killed.

The vast tomb of Emperor Qin Shi Huang (259–210 BC), at Lintong, in Shaanxi Province, was filled with an army of 8,000 soldiers, 130 chariots and 670 horses. All the figures were life-size and made of terracotta. The figures were found by accident in 1974, and are now a major tourist attraction.

Railways dominate the long-distance transport network in China. There are 56,500 miles (91,000 km) of track, carrying 1.68 billion passengers each year, plus a huge volume of freight. Trains on the inter-city routes can travel at speeds over 186 mph (300 km/h).

AMAZING!

Peanuts

China is the world's largest producer of peanuts, growing over 14 million tonnes (15 million tons) each year – more than 40% of world production. Most of the crop is grown around the lower Huang Ho.

Southern China

South of the Qin Mountains China has a climate that is warm and wet enough for rice to be grown easily.

The landscape is more rugged than in the north, with numerous ranges of hills and mountains cut by river valleys and gorges. Although political power is traditionally located in northern China, southern China has long been more prosperous and economically more important.

The largest city in China, with 23 million people, is Shanghai, near the mouth of the Yangtze River (Chang Jiang). In 1842 foreign merchants were allowed to settle in Shanghai, after which the city became China's main export port – a position it still holds.

In 2012, the Three Gorges Dam was completed on the Yangtze River. The dam holds back a massive lake. Water from the lake is used to generate hydroelectricity and irrigate fields. More than 1 million people had to be moved to make way for the lake.

SHANGHAI

Happy Journey

The Yangtze River flows for 3,915 miles (6,300 km) across southern China from the Tibetan Plateau to the Pacific Ocean. The river provides irrigation water for surrounding fields, and has long been an important transport route. Ocean ships can travel upriver for 620 miles (1,000 km).

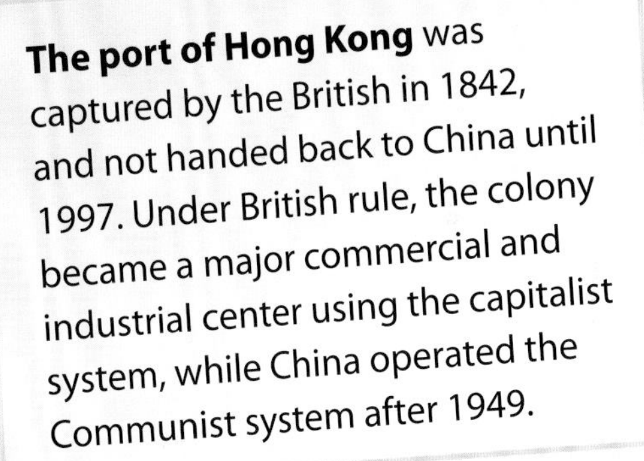

The port of Hong Kong was captured by the British in 1842, and not handed back to China until 1997. Under British rule, the colony became a major commercial and industrial center using the capitalist system, while China operated the Communist system after 1949.

AMAZING!

Pollution on the Yangtze

Since the 1950s, the Yangtze and its tributaries have been blocked by numerous dams and other works. The massive growth in industry since the 1980s has added pollution to the problems caused by the disrupted water flow, and in 2006 the Yangtze river dolphin became extinct.

Myanmar, Thailand, Cambodia, Laos, Vietnam

Southeast Asia

Southeast Asia, sometimes called Indo-China, is the part of Asia that lies between India and China.

In the past it included the Malay Peninsula, but that is now part of the country of Malaysia and is usually not included. The area has a hot, wet, tropical climate and rugged landscape.

The Mekong River flows for 2,703 miles (4,350 km) from the Tibetan plateau in China, through Myanmar (Burma), Laos, Thailand, Cambodia and Vietnam. The six countries co-operate on planning new dams and canals along the river to enhance trade and protect rare animals.

Traditional Cambodian apsara dance is performed to the sound of drums, cymbals and gongs. The slow, graceful movements of the elaborately dressed dancers symbolize religious or historical events.

Happy Journey

Rice may first have been cultivated 9,000 years ago. It is the single most important food in much of Asia. Rice plants are planted in paddy fields (flooded parcels of land), often terraced into steep hillsides. In most places harvesting is done by hand.

Ha Long Bay in northern Vietnam is a large bay dotted with thousands of small islands. The islands are home to many rare species of animals and plants. The bay has become a major tourist attraction.

PADDY FIELD

The vast temple of Angkor Wat in Cambodia is the world's largest religious monument. The complex was begun by the Khmer ruler Suryavarman II in about 1140, with changes and additions continuing for four centuries.

Malaysia

The country of Malaysia was formed in 1963 when the countries of Malaya, Sabah and Sarawak joined together.

The countries shared a common Islamic religion and Malay culture, although about one-quarter of the population is Chinese in origin. The area was, for years, ruled by Britain, and now has a system of government modeled on that of Britain.

The Malayan gharial, or false gharial, is a freshwater relative of the crocodile native to Peninsular Malaysia, Sarawak, Sumatra and Borneo. There are thought to be fewer than 2,500 adults surviving.

The twin Petronas Towers in Malaysia's capital, Kuala Lumpur, stand 451.9 m (1,483 ft) tall and were the tallest buildings in the world from 1998 to 2004. The towers are occupied by offices, half of which belong to the Petronas oil company.

The Masjid Negara, or National Mosque of Malaysia, in Kuala Lumpur, is one of the largest in Asia – it can hold 15,000 people. Its was built from glass and concrete in 1965, and has 48 small domes plus a main dome that resembles a semi-opened umbrella.

Data Bank

Area
127,354 square miles (329,847 sq km)

Population
28,334,000

Produce per person
$16,942

Highest point
Mt Kinabalu, 4,095 m (13,435 ft)

Murtabak is a popular breakfast dish in Malaysia, where it is sold from street stalls. It is a pancake wrapped around a stuffing of chopped mutton, garlic, egg and fried onions.

MURTABAK

Kuala Lumpur is located where the Klang and Gombak rivers meet – its name literally means "muddy confluence." Chinese tin miners founded the city in 1857. Since then it has grown to become one of the major trading centers of Southeast Asia. The city is the official residence of the Malaysian king.

Happy Journey

Indonesia

Indonesia is an archipelago, or island chain, comprising approximately 17,508 islands between Asia and Australia.

It was formed in December 1949, when it became independent of the Netherlands, which had ruled for the previous 300 years. The people of the islands share the Islamic religion, but have quite distinct cultures and languages.

Data Bank

Area 735,358 square miles (1,904,569 sq km)

Population 237,424,000

Product per person $4,977

Highest point Puncak Jaya, 4,884 m (16,024 ft)

In the wild, orangutans live only in the forests of Borneo and Sumatra. They feed on fruits, leaves, shoots, insects and eggs. There are thought to be about 70,000 left, but the population is declining due to the forests being cleared.

AMAZING!

The huge Suramadu Bridge links the islands of Java and Madura. Completed in 2009, it is 3.4 miles (5.4 km) long and has a central span of 818 m (2,684 ft).

DID YOU KNOW?

The Istiqlal Mosque in Jakarta, Indonesia's capital, is the largest mosque in Southeast Asia. Its courtyard can hold 120,000 people. The central dome is 45 m (148 ft) across – the number "45" symbolizing the 1945 proclamation of Indonesia's independence.

ISTIQLAL MOSQUE

Paddy field

On Java, shadow puppets are hugely popular. The flat puppets are manipulated by rods. The performer sits behind a screen and uses the puppets to cast shadows that can be seen by the audience on the other side of the screen.

Philippines

The Philippines are a group of more than 7,000 islands to the north of Indonesia.

Many of the islands are steep, rugged and volcanic – there are 50 volcanoes in all, 20 of which are considered active. The climate is tropical, with hot temperatures and heavy rainfall. The isolated position of the islands means that much of the wildlife is unique to this country.

Manila, the capital, is the most densely populated city on Earth, with 1.7 million people packed into just 15 square miles (39 sq km). In 1571 the Spanish made it their base for the Spanish conquest of the islands. Today, 97% of the population are Christian.

Basketball is one of the most popular pasttimes in the Philippines. The game was introduced by the United States, which ruled the country from 1898 to 1946.

At festivals, Filipinos often eat a dish called kare-kare. An oxtail and tripe are boiled until tender. Then rice, banana shoots, peanuts, beans and cabbage are added to create a thick stew.

Data Bank

Area
115,831 square miles
(300,000 sq km)

Population
97,703,000

Product per person
$2,614

Highest Point
Mount Apo, 2,954 m
(9,692 ft)

NO LEFT TURN

AMAZING!

Every January, a great festival is held to honor the Philippines' holiest relic, a small statue of the baby Jesus, called Santo Niño de Cebú. In 1521 it was given to a local lady by the Portuguese explorer, Ferdinand Magellan.

Coconut oil is one of the more important exports of the Philippines. It is extracted from coconuts that have been dried in the sun, and can be stored for up to two years. The oil is used in cooking in the Philippines and other tropical countries.

Australasia and Oceania

Australasia is the name for Australia and the areas around it, including New Zealand and Papua New Guinea. Oceania is a region that includes Australasia and the 30,000 or so islands dotted across the vast Pacific Ocean.

Kimberley was one of the earliest settled parts of Australia. People first landed, probably from the islands of Indonesia, about 41,000 years ago. It has a tropical monsoon climate, with about 90% of its rain falling between November to April.

VISAS 11

Stats and Facts

Countries:
Australia, New Zealand, Micronesia, Palau, Papua New Guinea, Solomon Islands, Vanuatu, Fiji, Tonga, Samoa, Nauru, Marshall Islands, Kiribati, Tuvalu

Largest City:
Sydney, Australia, 4.6 million people

Tallest Mountain:
Mt Wilhelm, Papua New Guinea, 4,509 m (14,793 ft)

Longest River:
Murray River, Australia 1,572 miles (2,530 km)

The dynamic city of Sydney is the commercial, financial and cultural heart of Australia. Its most famous landmarks are the Sydney Opera House and the Sydney Harbour Bridge.

At Alice Springs, in the center of Australia, temperatures reach 45°C (113°F) and rainfall is low. Life is only possible because the town has springs of fresh water.

Referred to as the "Sunshine State," Queensland is home to 10 of Australia's 30 largest cities, located mainly along the coast.

The Great Barrier Reef lies off the northeast coast of Australia. It stretches for 1,600 miles (2,600 km) north to south, and is visited by 2 million people each year.

During the Ice Ages, the sea levels of the world were lower and Australia was linked to Tasmania and New Guinea by dry land. Animals, plants and people were able to walk from one landmass to the other. Australia remained separated by deep sea from the rest of Asia, however.

Habitats and Wildlife

Australasia has a wide range of climates. Much of Australia is hot and dry, with rainfall plentiful only in the southeast.

Some of the islands are new volcanic masses with fertile soils, while others are composed of ancient rocks and are almost barren.

SCAN ME

Instructions on page 5

The saltwater crocodile can crush the skull of a cow with ease and can easily eat a human. It is the largest reptile in the world, growing up to 6 m (20 ft) long. In Australia, the biggest populations are clearly signed, but they still manage to kill an average of two people a year.

RAINFOREST

Dense tropical rainforest covers the Cape York Peninsula in northeastern Australia. Rainforest creatures include 200 species of butterfly, and the northern quoll – a forest marsupial now low in numbers because it eats the introduced poisonous cane toad.

Fiordland is the mountainous area along the southwestern coast of New Zealand's South Island. It is covered in dense forest and has poor soils unsuitable for farming, so hardly anyone lives there.

FIORDLAND, NEW ZEALAND

The takahe is an extremely rare New Zealand bird, thought to have been extinct until 1948, when several were seen in the Murchison Mountains. The bird is now strictly protected and its habitat is being conserved.

AMAZING!

Marsupials are a group of mammals that were once widespread across the world, but are now restricted to Australasia and South America. Baby marsupials develop in a pouch of skin on their mother's belly.

Deserts cover nearly one-fifth of Australia. Rainfall averages about 150 mm (6 in.) per year, while daytime temperatures can hit 50°C (122°F).

Peoples

The peoples of Australasia are a very mixed group.

The indigenous peoples are divided into a large number of groups and tribes. Europeans started arriving about 230 years ago, bringing with them their own cultures and lifestyles. More recently, people from Asia have been moving into the region.

Polynesians live on about 1,000 islands in the central and southern Pacific, in a triangular area linking New Zealand, Easter Island and the Hawaiian Islands. There are about 2 million Polynesians.

POLYNESIAN

Chinese immigrants to Australia established Chinatowns in several major cities, such as Sydney, Brisbane and Melbourne. In New Zealand, Asians or their descendants make up about 9% of the population, and in Australia it's about 12%.

Largescale European settlement began in the late 18th century. Europeans brought their livestock, culture and religion with them. About 85% of Australians and 78% of New Zealanders are descended from European settlers.

AMAZING!

Melanesians

The Melanesians live on the large island of New Guinea, and the smaller islands to the east and southeast as far as Fiji and Norfolk Island. The major islands include New Caledonia, Vanuatu, the Solomons, Bougainville, Santa Cruz, the Bismarck Archipelago and the Loyalty Islands.

MICRONESIANS

The Micronesians live on the islands north of New Guinea and east of the Philippines. These include the Caroline Islands, the Gilbert Islands, the Mariana Islands, the Marshall Islands, Nauru and Wake Island.

Beautiful Australia

The Aborigines of Australia are the descendants of the original humans who arrived in Australia about 60,000 years ago. They followed a hunter-gatherer lifestyle. Today, most Aboriginals live and work on farms or in towns. They have a rich tradition of dance, storytelling, rock painting and engraving.

Australia
The cities

Australia has become one of the most urbanized countries in the world, with 89% of people living in cities, mostly around the coast.

Sydney is centered around the vast natural inlet of Sydney Harbour. It was settled by the British in 1788, and was the first permanent European settlement in the region. Today it is a center for financial services, banks and the stock exchange. Sydney has a vibrant arts culture, too, and hosts numerous international sporting events.

CANBERRA

Canberra was chosen to be the capital of the new Commonwealth of Australia in 1901. Its economy is based almost entirely on the business of government, run from Parliament House.

Data Bank

Area of Australia
2,969,907 square miles
(7,692,024 sq km)

Population
23,032,797

Product per person
$65,642

Highest point
Mt Kosciuszko, 2,228 m
(7,310 ft)

Perth is the largest city in Western Australia – it has a population of 1.8 million. The vast mineral wealth of Western Australia means that the economy of Perth is dominated by businesses operating mines and quarries, or involved with processing minerals.

AMAZING!

The Adelaide Festival is the leading arts and culture event in Australia. It showcases films, theater, books, painting, cabaret and a host of other genres. The Festival was first held in Adelaide in 1960.

Melbourne, in the far southeast, enjoys a warm and varied climate. In recent years, biotechnology and computer sciences have become increasingly important here. The city also hosts the famous Melbourne Cup, a popular horse race shown on TV throughout Australia.

Australia

Farming and animals

Australia is famous for its huge sheep farms. Farmers also raise dairy and beef cattle, and grow wheat, rice, fruit and vegetables. Crops are mostly grown in the southeast.

Kangaroos are native to Australia and are found nowhere else. They bound across the grassy plains, stopping to graze on grass or browse on shrubs. Larger kangaroos can keep hopping for over 1 hour, at up to 15 mph (25 km/h).

The Darling and Murray rivers flow across mostly dry plains. Most of their water comes from rain that falls in hills to the east, and is used to irrigate food crops. The two rivers join before entering the sea.

Happy Journey

AMAZING!

Darwin, on the north coast, has a population of 129,000. In 1974 it was almost totally destroyed by Cyclone Tracey, which flattened 80% of the city. Darwin exists largely to handle overseas trade to and from the Northern Territory.

Australia is the fourth-largest exporter of wine, shipping 750 million litres (198 million gallons) abroad each year. The export trade has been built up since the 1970s, when producers started to make big improvements to quality and consistency.

Wombats are large marsupials that grow up to 1 m (3 ft) long. They are most common in Tasmania and southeastern Australia, where they feed at night or around dusk on grass, roots, shoots and bark.

KOALAS

AMAZING!

Koalas live in eucalyptus forests – eucalyptus leaves are the only food they will eat. Until the 1920s they were hunted for their fur, and nearly became extinct. However, conservation measures were successful and they are now numerous.

Wool is big business in Australia. The country produces about 25% of the world's output. Nearly all of it is Merino wool, which is fine and soft. The vast majority of Australian wool is used to make quality clothing.

New Zealand

The islands of New Zealand lie about 930 miles (1,500 km) east of Australia.

The two largest islands are North Island and South Island, which together make up more than 90% of the land area. When Europeans arrived in New Zealand, it was already inhabited by the Maori people – eastern Polynesian settlers who arrived some time between 800 and 1300.

WELLINGTON

AMAZING!

Maori crafts, particularly woodwork, are much in demand. The Maori developed their own distinctive culture partly because they were cut off from other Polynesians by hundreds of miles of sea.

Wellington, on North Island, is the capital of New Zealand – and the southernmost capital city in the world. This compact city is New Zealand's political center. It has a lively arts scene, as well as film and theater industries.

Mount Cook, also known as Aoraki, is the highest mountain in New Zealand. It is at the center of a national park that contains 140 high peaks and 72 glaciers, and has become a major tourist attraction.

The haka is a traditional dance performed by Maori when meeting people from another tribe, celebrating a success or when about to do battle. Sports teams from New Zealand often perform a haka before a game.

Data Bank

Area
103,483 square miles (268,021 sq km)

Population
4,451,000

Highest point
Mount Cook 3,754 m (12,316 ft)

Product per person
$27,666

MAORI TATTOO

Tattoos are especially elaborate in Maori culture. Maori men decorate their faces and bodies with swirls, spirals and intricate patterns. The moko was a special form of tattoo in which grooves were cut into the skin. Since the 1990s, there has been a revival in moko as Maori reassert their heritage.

AMAZING!

The kiwi is a flightless bird found only on New Zealand, and is a national symbol. "Kiwi" has become a nickname for people from the country. The islands have no native mammals, apart from bats.

Melanesia

The islands of Melanesia lie to the northeast of Australia.

The countries are Fiji, Papua New Guinea, the Solomon Islands and Vanuatu. Also included are New Caledonia, which belongs to France, and the western half of New Guinea, which is part of Indonesia. The islands are very mountainous, giving rise to a large number of almost isolated human populations. There are estimated to be about 1,300 different languages spoken across Melanesia.

The Fijian islands were part of the British Empire until 1970. English is still widely spoken and many features of public life are based on British models. Although usually grouped with Melanesia, the Fijians have several cultural links to Polynesia.

HINDU TEMPLE

The Sri Siva Subramaniya Temple at Nadi in Fiji is the largest Hindu temple south of the Equator. About 40% of Fiji's population are descended from Indians, who moved to the island during the 19th century to work on sugar plantations.

The balmy climate, spectacular scenery and unusual cultures of Melanesia offer great potential. However, transport problems, lack of investment and allegations of corruption have hindered developments.

Scuba diving is the mainstay of the tourist industry on the Solomon Islands, where the reefs are pristine and are said to be among the best in the world for divers. Many visitors stay in eco-lodges or village guest houses.

SCUBA DIVING

Mount Yasur on the island of Tanna in Vanuatu is one of the most active volcanoes in the region. The volcano is a tourist draw, but is frequently closed to visitors due to eruptions taking place.

Rainbow lorikeets

Micronesia

Although the islands of Micronesia are spread across a vast area, their combined land area is only 475 square miles (1,230 sq km).

Micronesia includes the Caroline Islands (Palau and the Federated States of Micronesia), the Gilbert Islands, most of which belong to Kiribati, the Mariana Islands (including Guam), the independent Marshall Islands, the island nation of Nauru, and Wake Island (a US territory).

Rai stones are used on Yap as a form of money, exchanged at marriages, peace agreements after war or as part of trade agreements. They vary in size from 7 cm (3 in.) to 3.6 m (12 ft).

The four islands of Yap have a population of 6,300. People work mainly on farms or fishing. Past rulers of Yap include Spain, Germany and Japan.

MANTA RAY

AMAZING!

The reefs are a big attraction for visitors, but getting to the islands is difficult because they are too small for modern jet airliners. Instead visitors must arrive by small aircraft. Despite these problems, visitor numbers have increased steadily since the mid 1990s.

The Parliament building on Kiribati is built of concrete and other modern materials, but in the shape of a traditional log house. The islands were for some years part of the British Empire, and Kiribati remains a member of the Commonwealth, although it has become a republic.

KIRIBATI PARLIAMENT HOUSE

PHOSPHATES, NAURU

The Bokikokiko is a warbler found only on the island of Kiribati. Because the Micronesian islands are so isolated, many of its birds and a few mammals and reptiles are unique to the islands.

Mining for phosphates in Nauru began in 1906. The mining caused extensive environmental damage. Chronic political instability has held back economic development, and Nauru is one of the poorest countries in the world. Unemployment hit 90% in 2006.

Polynesia

The outrigger canoe is the traditional Polynesian sea craft – the canoe has a side float attached by wooden poles. Polynesians used outrigger canoes to travel vast distances between the islands, sometimes staying afloat for months at a time.

Polynesia covers a vast area of the Pacific Ocean. The people on the scattered islands are Polynesians.

The islands have a shared culture rather than any geographic or geological link. Roughly speaking, the area occupies a triangle with New Zealand at the southwestern corner, Easter Island in the southeast and Hawaii in the north. Apart from New Zealand, the islands lie in the tropics, giving Polynesia a shared set of agricultural plants.

DID YOU KNOW?

King George Tupou V was Tonga's flamboyant king from 2006 to 2012. He launched an era of democracy on Tonga. Traditionally, Polynesian society was organized under chiefs. Most of Polynesia has abandoned this system as it was linked to the native religions.

AMAZING!

Rapa Nui, or Easter Island, marks the far point of Polynesian expansion. It was settled about the year AD 900. The settlers erected hundreds of stone statues, up to 10 m (33 ft) tall, to celebrate famous ancestors. The statues were later overthrown, perhaps as a result of civil war or a revolution.

EASTER ISLAND HEADS

DANCE

Dance has long been an important feature of Polynesian culture. Different dances symbolize welcome, hostility or triumph, and are performed at major social events or family celebrations.

Hawaii is now a US state. The population of 1.4 million is about 10% native Hawaiian, 25% white, 39% Asian and 24% mixed. The vast majority of non-Hawaiians were born elsewhere or are descended from people who moved here after the USA took over the islands in 1898.

Antarctica

The extreme north and south of the Earth are bitterly cold. They receive little heat from the sun, even in midsummer, and in winter are plunged into darkness lasting weeks on end.

The South Pole lies in the center of Antarctica, a continent that remains below freezing for most of the year, and is largely covered by snow and ice.

Parts of Antarctica are claimed by: Britain, New Zealand, France, Norway, Australia, Chile, Argentina, South Africa, the United States and Russia.

VISAS 11

Stats and Facts

Area
5.4 million square miles (14 million sq km)

Population
nil

Highest Point
Mount Erebus, 3,794 m (12,448 ft)

POLO NORTE
URUGUAY
VALPARAISO
JAPON
ARAUCO
KOREA
AUSTRALIA
CHUE
ANTARTICA

DID YOU KNOW?

Minerals on Antarctica
Antarctica is known to have extensive deposits of coal and iron ore, and large oil and gas fields lie under the Ross Sea. An international treaty bans the removal of any mineral deposits in Antarctica until 2024.

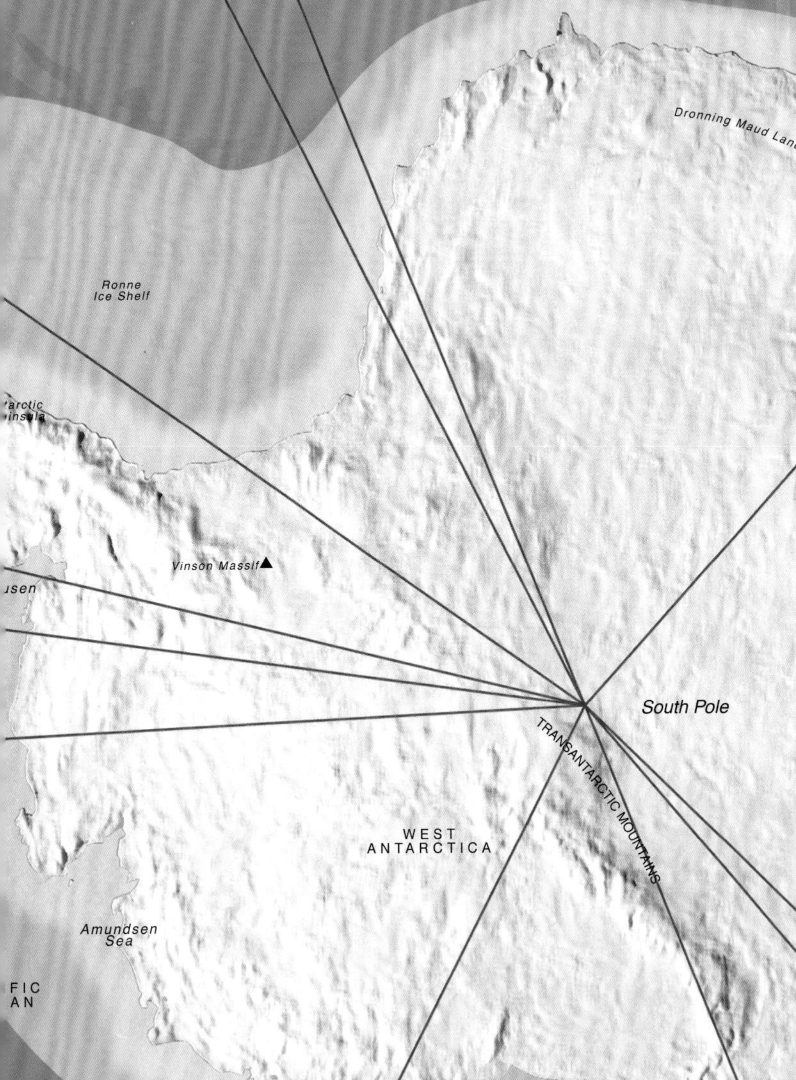

Dronning Maud Land

Ronne
Ice Shelf

Vinson Massif

South Pole

TRANSANTARCTIC MOUNTAINS

WEST
ANTARCTICA

Amundsen
Sea

Ross
Ice Shelf

Victoria
Land

South
Magnetic
Pole

AMUNDSEN

The first person to reach the South Pole was the Norwegian explorer Roald Amundsen. He arrived there in December 1911, followed five weeks later by the British explorer Robert Scott.

RESEARCH

Scientific research stations on Antarctica are occupied by visiting scientists. There are about 5,000 in the summer, dropping to about 1,000 in winter. No one lives permanently on Antarctica.

Habitats and Wildlife

AMAZING!

Penguins live mostly on Antarctica, but also on the nearby islands and the south coasts of South America, Africa and Australasia. They are unable to fly, but are superb swimmers. There are 17 species of penguin living in the southern hemisphere. These Adélie penguins live on Antarctica's Ross Island.

The geographic South Pole is on a high plateau 2,835 m (9,301 ft) above sea level. The plateau is covered in ice more than 1.6 km (1 mile) thick.

The ice is moving at a rate of about 10 m (33 ft) per year, so the signpost marking the South Pole has to be moved each year for its position to remain accurate.

Mount Erebus is the tallest mountain in Antarctica. It reaches 3,794 m (12,447 ft). It's the most active volcano on the continent, and also one of the most active on Earth – it has been erupting continuously since 1972.

FASCINATING FACTS

- Antarctica is considered a desert because it gets so little rain.
- The coldest recorded temperature on Earth occurred at Vostok Station, Antarctica, in 1983. It measured -89.2°C (-128.6°F).
- "Antarctica" comes from a Greek word meaning "opposite to the north."

Of the 36 seal species, only six live on Antarctica – Antarctic fur seals (shown here), crabeater seals, leopard seals, Ross seals, Weddell seals and southern elephant seals. With no natural land predators, such as polar bears, Antarctic seals show little fear of people.

AMAZING!

The orca, or killer whale, lives in both Arctic and Antarctic waters (as well as other oceans and seas). It lives in pods of up to 25 individuals, which co-operate with each other when hunting for prey, such as seals.

ORCA

The Arctic

The North Pole lies in the middle of the Arctic Ocean.

The ocean is largely surrounded by land, and on the sea bed an underwater range of mountains, named the Lomonosov Ridge, runs from Siberia to Canada. The combination of the ridge and the encircling land stops warm currents from farther south reaching the Arctic, so the surface of the sea stays largely frozen in winter and only partly thaws in the summer. There are a few scattered human populations on the fringes of the polar regions, but none at the Pole itself.

Data Bank

Area
5,427,051 square miles (14,056,000 sq km)

Population
None, but some settlements on the coasts

Deepest point
Litke Deep , 5,450 m (17,880 ft)

The Svalbard island group in the Arctic is the northernmost part of Norway. It has a population of 2,642 – a mixture of Norwegians, Russians, Ukrainians and a few Poles. Mining, research and tourism are the main industries.

Global warming is causing the Arctic ice to melt at an alarming rate. The yellow line shows the extent of the sea ice in 1979–2000, the green line shows it in 2005 and the red line shows the 2007 ice limit.

AMAZING!

Oil and gas
Vast oil and gas fields lie under the Arctic Ocean. There are competing claims from countries with coasts on the Ocean. Drastic melting of the glaciers makes exploitation of the mineral deposits more likely.

American Frederick Cook claimed that, on 21 April 1908, he and two Inuit men were the first people to reach the North Pole. However, he later lost his navigational records and so was unable to prove anything.

The United States (Alaska)

Canada

North Pole

Russia

Greenland (Denmark)

Norway (Svalbard)

Arctic Circle

SOUTH POLE

ROBERT PEARY, 1909

American Robert Peary claimed he reached the North Pole on 6 April, 1909, but recent study of his records has cast doubt on whether he was where he thought he was. On 10 May, 1926, Norwegian Roald Amundsen got to the North Pole by airship, a claim that nobody disputes.

Habitats and Wildlife

The land within the Arctic Circle is mostly covered by tundra. The weather is so cold, and the summers so short, that very little vegetation can grow. There are no trees at all and ground cover is generally made up of moss, lichen, grass or small shrubs.

Despite the extreme cold, persistent winds and short growing season, many animals have adapted to live in the severe environment of the Arctic.

Sea ice forms when the air temperature drops below freezing for a long time. Where the ice is attached to a coast it is known as fast ice, while drift ice is free to move with the currents.

The Arctic wolf is almost identical to a normal gray wolf, but its coat is white instead of grey and it can grow to be slightly larger. It preys on musk oxen and reindeer in cold northern Canada and Greenland.

ARCTIC WOLF

DID YOU KNOW?

Greenland is covered by a vast central ice sheet, in places almost 2 miles (3 km) thick. In several places the ice moves down to the sea in glaciers, which constantly break off to form icebergs. One of these icebergs famously sank the passenger ship *Titanic* in 1912.

SCAN ME

Instructions on page 5

POLAR BEAR

AMAZING!

The musk ox is native to Canada and Greenland, and small populations have been introduced to Siberia and Norway. This hefty animal has a soft undercoat and a coarse, long outer coat to keep it warm.

The great hunter of the Arctic is the polar bear. It spends more than half its time hunting, mainly for ringed and bearded seals because it needs large amounts of fat to survive.

Index

Picture credits

tr = top right; br = bottom right; tl = top left; bl = bottom left; tc = top centre; bc = bottom centre; lc = left centre rc = right centre; c = centre; main = main image

p6, c. NASA/CXC/M.Weiss; X-ray: NASA/CXC/UC Berkeley/N.Smith et al.; IR: Lick/UC Berkeley/J.Bloom & C.Hansen, p7, br. Roger Stewart; p12, bl. NASA, p12, br. KVDP; p15, bl. U.S. Navy; p15, bl. NOAA, p15, br. officer or employee of the United States Government as part of that person's official duties; p16/17, map. Roger Stewart; p20, bl. Ansgar Walk; p23, br. Ansgar Walk; p31, tl. Parkerjh; p33, map. Roger Stewart; p35 tl. Dominio público, Thinkstock; p39, bl. Dabackgammonator, tl. Gerardo Gonzalez, tr. Mastretta; p56, map. Roger Stewart, cl. Bjørn Christian Tørrissen; p63, br. Juliux; p65, Map. Roger Stewart; p72, bl. Web Gallery of Art; p76, tr. Bikerboy-93, p77, tl. Jpatokal, cr. Mgiganteus, p82, map. Roger Stewart; p86, tr. PD-Eigen; p95, tr. NASA, p94/95, main. Andy Waite, p96/97, main. Paulo César Santos; p100, map. Roger Stewart; p103, cl. Becker0804; p105, cr. CC-Zero; p114, tr. David Raykovitz; p117, tr. Lisa Coghlan, bl. Muhammad Mahdi Karim; p120/121, map. Roger Stewart; p128, tr. Mai-Linh Doan; p130, cr. Felice Beato; p146/147, map. Roger Stewart; p149, cl. Maungatautari Ecological Island Trust; p150, cl. Marcus Wong; p161, cl. CdaMVvWgS, tr. jopolopy, br DickDaniels; p162, bl. PD-USGOV, p164/165, map. Roger Stewart, tr. Olav Bjaaland, p166, bl. Richard Waitt, U.S. Geological Survey; p168, cl. NASA scientist Joey Comiso, p169, map. Roger Stewart, bl. Robert Edwin Peary

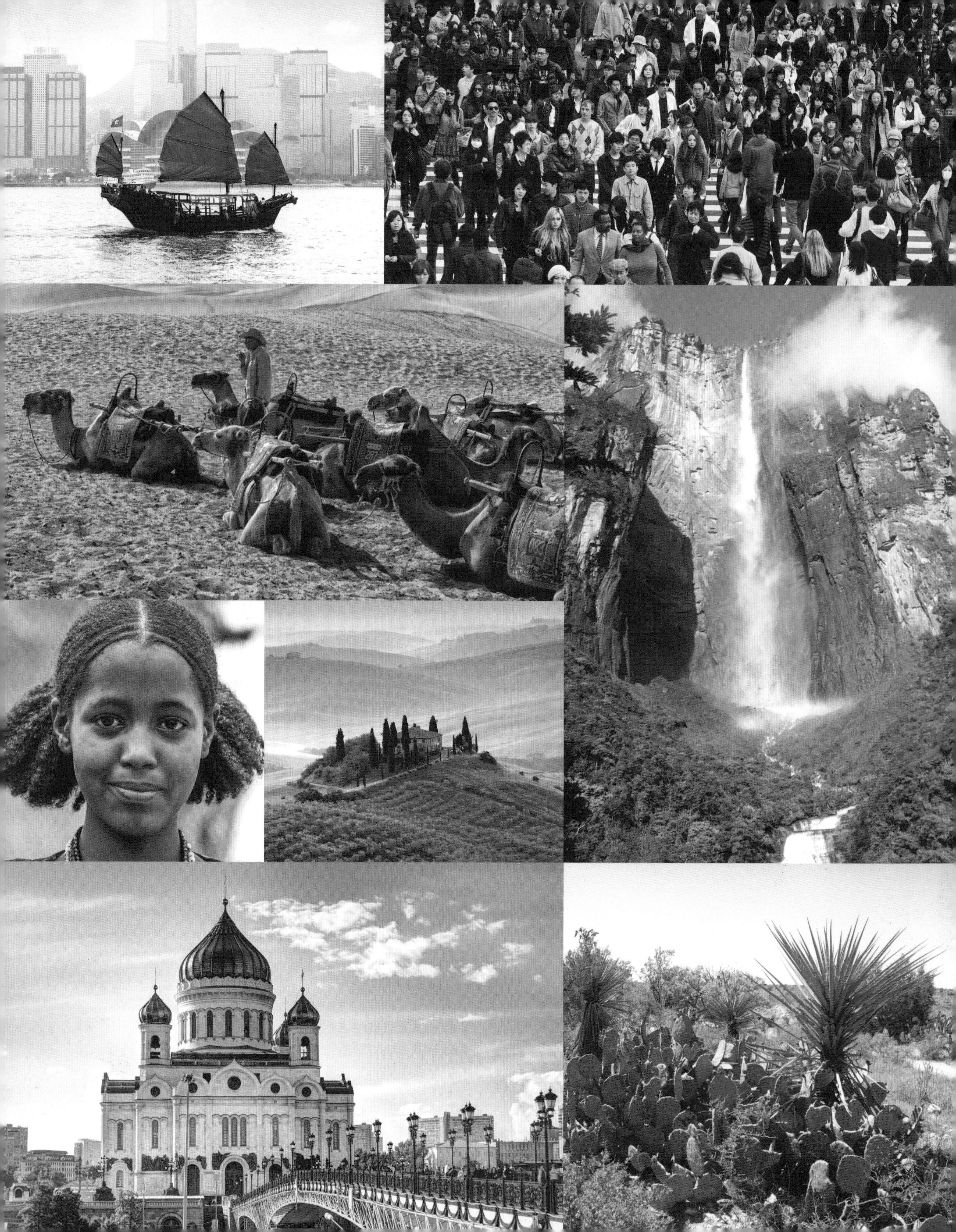